Tight Corners
In Pastoral Counselling

FRANK LAKE

Tight Corners
In Pastoral Counselling

Darton, Longman and Todd
London

First published in Great Britain in 1981
by Darton, Longman and Todd Ltd
89 Lillie Road, London SW6 IUD

© 1981 Frank Lake

ISBN 0 232 51309 0

British Library Cataloguing in Publication Data

Lake, Frank
  Tight corners in pastoral counselling.
  1. Pastoral counselling
  I. Title
  253.5   BV4012.2

ISBN 0–232–51309–0

Phototypeset by Input Typesetting Ltd., London SW19 8DR.

Printed in Great Britain by the Anchor Press Ltd
and bound by Wm Brendon and Son Ltd
both of Tiptree, Essex.

Contents

Preface

This book has burst the table of contents originally intended for it. Eight years ago, Tim Darton, who had originally invited me to write the tome, *Clinical Theology*, which Darton, Longman and Todd published in 1966, asked for a sequel, a Training Manual which would bring the work up to date. That has still to come. This is something else.

During a four-month sabbatical and a four-month convalescence in 1977–8, I read a lot and reflected on my experience in the 'tight corners' of pastoral and psychiatric counselling. There are issues which are sharp enough as social problems, in marriage and the single life, in divorce, remarriage and same-sex loving, which become acutely painful when they have driven vulnerable individuals into breakdown. These were the concerns I had in mind when most of the present chapters were projected as essays into 'tight corners'.

In sending them two years ago to my patient publisher, now John Todd, I was aware of their lack of structure and coherence. Michael Jacobs, the student counsellor at Leicester University, kindly agreed to edit them. He did so and they began to flow in some sequence. In reading them for publication I realized that some were tight corners no longer or, if they remained tight, they were no longer dark corners.

New Light on Dark Corners

For most of my psychiatric life I have been working in a half-light, oblivious of the earliest and severest forms of human pain. We have always known, whether taught by St. Augustine, Søren Kierkegaard or Sigmund Freud, that infants suffered abysmally, and that human beings crawling out of their abysses into life have damaged perceptions, distorted goals and a lifetime bondage of primal fears. What we had not known, and even now are somewhat terrified to know as clearly and rigorously as in fact we do, is the contribution to this soul-destroying pain and heart-breaking suffering that comes from the distress of the foetus in the womb when the mother herself is distressed. *The focus for psychopathology is now, for us, the first trimester of intra-uterine life.* These first three months after conception hold more ups and downs, more ecstasies and devastations than we had ever imagined.

A New Stance

Where, then, does Clinical Theology stand nowadays? Our determination has always been to be sensitive to the interface between our own body of growing experience, theory and practice, and that of other secular and spiritual movements also engaged in counselling. This has led to changes in the structure and content of the seminars in human relations, pastoral care and counselling, and in the personal growth and integration workshops. Some changes have already taken effect, others are being built in. Since what is now changing has been of value to thousands of people, the direction of the changes and the reasons for making them should be made clear. I propose to discuss that in this preface.

From 1958 to 1981, over 12,000 men and women from all callings have gathered with a CT Tutor to study and practise pastoral counselling. In large and small towns throughout England, Wales and Scotland they have agreed to work together for twelve three-hour sessions in each year. For most of them this has been part of a two-year course, with relevant reading matter supplied. The amalgam of our activities is well known.

Many other counselling movements have grown up alongside us during these years, or continued in their longer history. Where, then, does the work reported here stand in relation, for instance, to the main-stream of psychoanalytically orientated counselling, or to the Rogerian school updated by R. R. Carkhuff and his associates? Where does it stand in relation to the main form of therapy that has been encouraged to expand in the National Health Service in the hands of the clinical psychologists, namely Behavioural Modi-

fication Therapy. This promises to be more scientific and cost-
effective than any but the briefest of psychotherapies. It also has a
natural background of scientific medical support. How is this reflected in recent neurophysiology, in the concepts of learning and
memory organized in holograms at the synapses, and learning associated with biochemical changes in protein molecular structures
within the cells?

CTA's Early Recognition of Peri-Natal Stress

Those who have benefited from a counselling course based on a
theory of origins stemming back to birth and the first year of life
may well be disturbed by the rumour that we now regard these as
not going back early enough. My psychiatric colleagues and I 'stuck
our necks out' twenty-three years ago in affirming birth and the
early months as powerfully relevant occasions of stress. I am grateful
to those who trusted our integrity in diving in at a deeper end than
most psychoanalysts could tolerate twenty years ago. Now, when
some Freudians are implicitly critical of the master, by taking birth
and maternal bonding seriously, we have had to push further back
still and follow the intuition opened up to us by 'deep-sea' fantasy
journeys, and recognise that life in the womb is a potent source of
psychopathology.

Recognition of Stress in the Womb

To shorten a long story, we have been led, step by step, to test this
intuition, to find means to enable people to make this retrospective
journey, and to develop techniques of contextualizing these 'primal'
experiences in the successive months of pregnancy. We find we
must begin at conception, through the blastocystic stage, to implantation and the events of the first trimester. It is here, in the
first three months or so of life in the womb, that we have encountered the origins of the main personality disorders and the psychosomatic stress conditions. Summarizing our findings in over one
thousand two hundred subjects who have relived the intra-uterine
journey during residential three to six-day workshops, we have
concluded that there exists what we have called the 'Maternal-
Foetal Distress Syndrome'.

This hypothesis, of a maternal-foetal affect flow, transmitted by the umbilical cord, has so far resisted our attempts to nullify it. So we advance the interpretive concept that the emotional state of the pregnant mother is transmitted to the foetus. Her joy and recognition of her changed state leads to foetal joy in being recognized, accepted and, indeed, welcomed. Her distress, if that is her condition during the first trimester, invades the foetus in the form of a bitter, black flood. This 'incompatible transfusion' of alien emotions leads to a variety of reactions in the foetus. It may cope with, or totally oppose it. The mode of the opposition varies with constitutional factors, intensities of stress and its duration, as well as with previous experiences severe enough to cause conditioned responses. If opposing the distress, in the name of life and growth, becomes too painful, and the prospect of betterment too slight or far off, the foetus may flip into the paradox of transmarginal stress. Overwhelmed by dread and affliction, the organism longs for oblivion and death. Too late to save the day, offers of life, warmth and affirmation are now painfully declined.

We were bold in the 1950s, in adopting the Pavlovian theory of Transmarginal Stress as applicable to babies undergoing intolerable desertion. We discerned the mirror images of hysterical and schizoid reactions as resultants of this stress. We still regard the Pavlovian interpretation of post-natal stress as correct. However, we now recognize that these discontinuous reactions, which disrupt personality when it is subjected to too-prolonged or too-severe stress, occur catastrophically in the first three months of life in the womb. Incidentally, there are now available mathematical models of these paradoxical reactions in what is termed 'catastrophe theory'. I find it hard to understand why Pavlov's findings have not been adopted by clinical psychologists and child psychologists. They explain so much that is otherwise quite baffling, particularly in those conditions which betray a wish to die, as strong or stronger than the willingness to live, and in the prevalent overlap of separation-anxiety and commitment-anxiety in the same person.

Behaviour Modification Theory and Therapy

The earlier manipulative methods associated with behavioural therapy relied, with scientific self-congratulation, on an impersonal, instrumental conditioning approach. The process utilized aversion, emphasizing unpleasant consequences, relying on reinforcement with extraneous rewards and punishments. Factual to the point of hardness, these methods did not prove applicable to groups of friends working to help each other. However, later developments of behaviour therapy have brought its theory and practice to the point where we can recognize, in its extended principles, what we are already doing.

In a recent summary of Behaviour Therapy as it applies to the diseases of stress (especially migraine headaches, asthma and proneness to coronary heart disease), Michael Spevack, addressing the Second International Symposium on the Management of Stress, emphasized that there are now three crucial elements.[1] These are:

1 *Training in relaxation techniques*: The adult is taught how to take steps to reduce the anxiety level. For example, he can engage in deep breathing, and wait for the panic, which is in part due to the suppression of breathing, to diminish as he does so. Of course, if he is using the panic attacks to engage the attention of someone his 'child' wishes to dominate he will plead some excuse why it does not work. Otherwise, it is in his power to take back control of himself, *to trust* more of the good air around him to lift him out of the airless pit.

2 *Training in worry-stopping techniques*: Those who attack themselves with negative talk, putting themselves down, are accentuating the severity of whatever current stress is working against them. Their own internal and self-generated stress factor may be much greater than the external, situational factors. Recognizing this, the behavioural therapist must somehow reduce this self-induced worrisomeness. Realistic, positive, adjustive, hopeful thinking brings about a less stressful adaptation to an unhelpful environment. So the cognitive task of understanding the origins of negative-suggestibility and attacks on self-worth becomes important to the behaviourist. No longer does he desire studiously to neglect it. Designing measures of cognitive value, such as positive, self-affirmative statements, which the subject can feed in to counteract the chronic, negative 'scripts', becomes a significant task in behavioural modification therapy.

Better thoughts and better images are well worth cultivating.

3 *Assertion training.* To be forced into anxious compliance to others increases the sense of being under intolerable stress. Bottling up

---

[1] *Stress*, vol. I, no. 4, pp. 6–12.

resentment uses up and, if it is not strictly necessary, actually wastes precious energy. To fear that some unthinkable catastrophe will occur, should a justly assertive anger burst out, is to live in a terrifying universe. The fear of the fear is usually much worse than is justified by the actual danger of the environment. By contrast, therefore, well-thought-out and rehearsed assertion, to re-establish justice in the personal interchange of power, significantly reduces the stress and the tension which the organism has to bear.

All three of these techniques of behaviour therapy are in essence, in our own Christian edition of them, an intrinsic part of what we already do in our workshops and are introducing in the seminars. This could endear us to the doctors, since behavioural therapies have a scientific reputation for firmer rationality and statistical reliability than psychoanalytic therapies.

A Move Away from Psychoanalytic Method

It seems that having travelled for 30 years in company with a psychoanalytically orientated counselling, we have moved decisively away from the desire to work by means of a strongly-developed one-to-one transference with the client. To offer interpretations based on the 'transference neurosis' is the last thing we do, in terms of classical Freudian, Kleinian, neo-Freudian or any other theory. Our task is to enable the subject to be in touch with his own pre- and peri-natal childhood memories so as to make his or her own connections, contextualizations and interpretations forward to current symptoms. We seek a therapeutic alliance as between co-operating adults. Parent-child transference feelings of dependency are obstacles to this. So we hand them back to the subject as too passive, as insufficiently relaxed, as muddled thinking about the task in hand. That attitude is lacking in the firm assertion of the 'adult' taking charge of his journey into his 'child's' world. The subject's own 'adult' *must* do the work of relating to their own 'child', otherwise no valid 'stitching' of the old tear can be done. A practised parental eagerness to do it for them can only get in their way. We have most trouble with those who have been too long in conventional therapy. We require a parity of power between us with which they have been rendered unfamiliar; as we believe, to their loss.

Back to the Early Freud and the Primary Process

In giving priority, as we do in this form of therapy, to the *discharge of excessive quantities of excitation* that have built up as a result of unmet primary needs, we are, by a strange irony, returning to Freud, the strict neurologist, and away from his later metapsychology and its aims and methods.

In 1895, Freud wrote to William Fliess: 'One evening last week when I was hard at work, tormented by just that amount of pain that seems to be the best state to make my brain function, the barriers were suddenly lifted, the veil was drawn aside, and I had a clear vision, from the details of the neuroses to the conditions that make consciousness possible.'

In particular, he distinguished the primary processes of the nervous system from the secondary. The primary function he saw as that by which neurons divest themselves of the unpleasurable quantities of excitation that have built up, for whatever reason, often the painful excitation due to unmet primary needs. This excitation, he recognized, was discharged 'through the motor systems, to neighbouring neural systems or through biological systems'. The use of each of these discharge routes had consequences which could lead to critical feedback. Motor discharge might hurt others and make matters worse; discharge into neighbouring systems generated other conflicts and led to divided attention; displacement into hormonal systems produced unpleasant kick-backs from the reaction of other hormones. So the drive of the primary process to reduce the load, by off-loading excessive parts of it, led to painful errors which had to be corrected by re-routing or containing it. The failure of the primary code of practice compelled the organism to decode it, and effect a recoding in terms of *compromise*.

This 'compromise tendency' Freud saw as a mixture of primary and secondary processes. The secondary process is based on the perception that the preferred discharge of unpleasurable excitation to zero by needs being met or protests heard is not proving possible in this constricted world of infant experience. The nervous system has to put up with a compromise by managing to *control a constant quantity of energy and excitation*. This involves setting up a programme of wishes, actions based on memories, balancing and judging between sets of alternatives. None of these can lead to the resting phase which the primary process envisaged when its excitation sought for safe conditions for a full discharge. So the secondary processes, the personality defences, and the fixed reaction patterns of a character adapted to the culture, must displace the primary hope for discharge from that war. Its substitute satisfactions are those of the perpetual juggler. The executive ego, residing in a consciousness which has lost contact with its roots, attempts to run the compromise with an eye to social survival.

For Freud, the task of therapy was to re-adjust the defensive tactics of the secondary process, to diminish the damage caused by operating outdated codes of emotional practice. He sought to maximize libidinal satisfactions within the bounds of cultural requirements considered as 'reality factors'. He regarded the primary process as inaccessible to therapy, as 'too hot' to work with safely.

For us, the primary process has become accessible to the subject's own insearch within a facilitating environment.

For Christians, the depth encounter of the Son of God, the image of the Father, with the exigencies of evil, led to the most violent discharges of rage and hate on the part of his accusers and executioners. In himself, according to Mark's account, the collison led in the end to a loud cry of total dereliction, followed by a yet louder cry of anguish as he died. This was the moment when the 'phase boundary' between God and man, 'the veil of the temple' was torn in two as the place of reconciliation was opened.

The depth counsellor is dealing with levels of excitation of comparable intensity in foetal persons near-aborted in destructive rage and spite, in births of brain-crushing cruelty and in new-born babies left derelict to fall to a death of the spirit in dread.

It is understandable that those who have no knowledge of the cost to God of redemptive intervention by identifying with our race should decide to work on the secondary process level, striving in consciousness to modify the more disabling misperceptions and reactions, leaving the primary catastrophes well alone. As those who have been drawn to faith in Christ, we do know the cost to God of encouraging us to *discharge* our deepest rage and spite on him and of his then inviting us to come back to him to have those needs fully met, to have our thirst quenched and, in place of emptiness, 'rivers of living water' flowing into and from the inward parts. To remain at the level of secondary process is to stay on the level of life under the law. In Christ, we have been made free and responsible to stay with each other while painful and angry exci-

tations are being thoroughly discharged. There is no merit in bottling them up, indeed that has become a form of faithlessness. It
leads, not to health but to internalized tension and the diseases of
stress.

*Long-term Memory Based in the Synaptic Microstructure of the Cortex,
According to a Holographic Principle.*

In *Languages of the Brain* (Brooks/Cole, Monterey, Ca., 1971), Karl
H. Pribram has shown that long-term memory is based in the
slow-potential synaptic microstructure of the cerebral cortex. The
functional unit here is the neural junction, not the neuron. Neurons
do not replicate themselves, which gives no basis for long-term
memory. The neural junctions or synapses 'not only multiply; they
are also replete with active chemical processes, any or many of
which are candidates for the evanescent, temporary, and long term
modification upon which memory must be based'. As soon as synapses are present in the embryonic and foetal cortex, remembering
can begin.

Pribram has shown the significance of the properties of holograms, operating at the synapses, 'making them potentially important in understanding brain function. First . . . the information
about a point in the original image is distributed throughout the
hologram, making the record resistant to damage. Each small part
of the hologram contains information from the entire original image
and therefore can reproduce it . . . The hologram has a fantastic
capacity to usefully (i.e., retrievably) store information.'

This takes the possibility of long-term memory as far back as to
the embryonic-foetal stage when the cortical cells become available.
What processes could subserve learning and memory in the zygote
and the blastocyst before and after implantation? We ask this because our subjects so consistently produce them. It seems that there
may be structures in the protein molecule of the single cell which
can do this. I understand that the synapses of the cortex are necessary for holographic process utilizing Fourier transforms, but that
similar but simpler recording is feasible on the basis of properties
resident in the protein molecule.

The principle of *multilevel redundancy* provides for the reduplication
of the genetic material of the original zygote into the nucleus of
every cell of the body. Could there be reduplication and transfer of

memory also in the cytoplasm? Apparently so. Richard Dryden, an embryologist writes, in *Before Birth* (Heinemann 1978), 'it is possible that the zygote contains information in addition to that stored in the nucleus. There is indeed evidence that the cytoplasm of the fertilized egg contains information that is essential to at least the early stages of development. . . There are several sites where cytoplasmic information may be stored. The abundant free ribosomes may carry developmental information.' 'The mechanism of protein synthesis lends itself to analysis by information theory, with . . . the ribosomes helping to convert the coded message into a protein molecule.'

The 'implicate order' opens up possibilities of micro-storage, inconceivable until recent years. My interest in the possible biological bases of pre-verbal memories is not to demonstrate the legitimate existence of our findings but to indicate their biological feasibility, and to guard against dismissive criticism based on antiquated neurology when they are reviewed.

Indebtedness

In writing this book and developing the hypothesis of intra-uterine personality determinants and influences, both in this book and beyond it, I have been aware of being led, as by an invisible guide, to the person or author who provided me with the next essential block I needed for my building. Serendipity and synchronicity became realities as I stretched out my hand and opened a book in a friend's library, or a colleague drew my attention to this or that article or idea. Others sparked off in me new connections or directions as I spoke with them. We may even have been travelling in opposite directions in the world of ideas and loyalties, so none of them must be held at all responsible for where I have arrived. So I am grateful to them and wish to express my indebtedness.

They are: John Bedford, Howard Belben, David Boadella, Lee Eliason, William Emerson, John Fletcher, Ted German, John Gravelle, Katy Hale, Brian Hawker, John Heron, Jill Holdcroft, Dennis Hyde, Alison Hunter, Ted Kettell, Karl Lachler, David and Janet Lake, Sylvia Lake, my ever alert and discriminating wife, Ronnie Laing, John Lehmann, Jean Liedloff, Judy Loach, Anne Long, Miller Mair, Hugh Millett, John Mollison, Roger Moss, Florence Nichols-Haines, Margarethe Novaes-Brepohl, Tom Oden,

Alix Pirani, B. J. Prashantham, Karl Pribram, Shirley Rawson, Esko Rintala, Talib Rothengätter, John Rowan, Bill Smith, Peter Trenchard, Riitta Vainio, Lena Wademaar-Tuulse, John Wagler, David Wasdell, John Wattis, Joan Wescott, Roger Williamson, John Wilson, David Wood, Martin Yeomans and Jim Hieronymus.

To those who have worked with me as facilitators in our workshops and on the house team at Lingdale, deeply committed to the pains and joys of this approach, I am particularly grateful to John Fletcher, Jill Holdcroft, Geoffrey Lindsay, David Dixon, Alison Newbigin, Judy Rosenberg, Heather Redshaw, and Liz Welch. I thank my patient secretary, Hope LeSueur. Lesley Riddle and Michael Jacobs have attended to different aspects of the editing with the encouragement and patience I need. I am a fortunate man.

Introduction

This title rests on a metaphor. In using metaphor we are 'speaking of one thing as if it were another'. Tight corners are physical places in which human beings feel constricted. What connection could corners, particularly 'tight' ones, have with counselling?

Aristotle believed that 'the greatest thing' was 'a command of metaphor'. Shelley talked of metaphor as 'a way of thinking and living; an imaginative projection of the truth'. Metaphors have powerful linking functions, bringing what were formerly fragmented bits into wholes that can then be comprehended as a single picture. For Coleridge, metaphors enrich language so that it conveys more than its mere content of fact, but conveys 'likewise the character, mood and intentions of the person' who is using it.

For I. A. Richards, metaphor is not just a literary matter, 'it deals with issues central to psychology and human functioning'. He warns, as Miller Mair notes, that 'a serious study of metaphor may plunge us into very deep psychological waters'. Donald Schuon gave detailed consideration to metaphor 'as a means of entering the unknown for invention and discovery'. Metaphors constitute 'programmes for exploring new situations'. For Miller Mair, to whom I am indebted for this understanding of the power and function of metaphor in the communications between counsellor and client, therapist and patient, metaphor reaches out 'for what is unknown but dimly sensed through the medium of some familiar aspect of the known'.[1]

Hawkes noted that the deliberate use of metaphor 'intensifies

[1] Miller Mair, *Metaphor for Living*. (Nebraska Symposium on Motivation 1976)

language's characteristic activity, and involves, quite literally, the creation of a "new" reality'. Metaphors are 'imagination in action'. As such they can free human beings or enslave them. They can be clarifying and reconciling. They can also induce false fears, create confusion, disorientation, and lead to reckless, ill-considered and violent action. Metaphors provide terrible tools for demagogues bent on driving men to their destruction, or are winged messengers of the love of God into the heart of man.

Among other matters, this book explores the origins of some of the most powerful metaphors in human language, those that derive from birth and childhood, and as we see now to be necessary, extending that study back through intra-uterine life to implantation in the womb and to conception itself. The concept of long-term memory as depending on the protein molecule in the single cell, not on elaborate neural connections, opens up these kinds of possibilities.

The groups we use to promote the freeing and growth of relationships into genuine respect, sharing and caring, can themselves be perceived as wombs, so that powerful metaphors derived from the ups and downs of an individual's life when in the womb press into his or her experience of the group. The womb-based metaphor distorts group life somehow, either by a magical enhancement of it or by an uncanny conviction that to stay in it a moment longer will be to perish in some half-imagined holocaust.

The phenomenon of 'transference', that bedevils our attempts to give 'tender loving care' and no more, that is the main diagnostic and therapeutic tool of psychoanalysis, and a more or less well-handled factor in all one-to-one counselling, is metaphor in action. Unwittingly the client imports into the relation with the helper his relationship to significant former objects from early in his or her life history. At first regarded as a nuisance, by 1912 Freud invented a good use for it. 'Finally', he wrote, 'every conflict has to be fought out in the sphere of transference.'

Otto Rank saw clearly that the analytic transference evoked the metaphors associated with birth.[2] The prospect of having to end the treatment and forgo the womb-like security of the daily hour would, he observed, evoke the traumata of birth which brought this patient's uterine existence to an end. Had Freud built on Rank's work,

---

[2] Otto Rank, *The Trauma of Birth*. New York, Warner Torch Books, 1934.

which initially he welcomed as 'the most important progress since the discovery of psychoanalysis', the door would have been opened to the recognition and analysis of metaphors from as far back as the first trimester, the three months following conception. Unfortunately for psychoanalysis and for the whole counselling movement that became 'psychoanalytically orientated', in 1924, Freud yielded to the protests of Abraham, Jones and others of the core group, inflaming his fear 'lest the whole of his life work be dissolved by the importance attached to the trauma of birth'. Turning against Rank he wrote to Abraham, 'I am getting further and further away from the birth trauma. I believe it will 'fall flat' if one doesn't criticize it too sharply, and then Rank, who I valued for his gifts and the great services he has rendered, will have learned a useful lesson.'[3] It were best to draw a curtain over the lesson the perceptive Rank would learn from that betrayal. The metaphors of parricide, Freud's fear of being displaced and metaphorically murdered by one of his sons, which caused him on two occasions to lose consciousness, took precedence over the metaphors sustaining the objective seeker after truth.

I think I shall not be proved wrong in foreseeing a significant enrichment of psychoanalysis and psychotherapy, in the accuracy and fit of the interpretations open to it, as to what is going on in the transference, as soon as the strength and penetrative capacity of early pre-natal experiences as a main source of our metaphors, of life and death and all kinds of distress, have been fully recognized and developed.

David Wasdell (of the Urban Church Project) and I have lately been sparking each other off in the recognition that the dynamics of the city congregation, hard pressed to survive the constriction and confusion of the age, are no longer yielding to institutional analysis based on interpersonal, post-natal models such as those developed by Bion, A. K. Rice and Pierre Turquet. David Wasdell perceived that the metaphors determining the congregation's response to the situation were defences first learnt in response to the constriction of birth. I think I have persuaded him that we must also look much earlier than that. The congregation, in fact, tends to demand of the pastoral team the total attention in looking after their needs that is characteristic, not of post-natal, interpersonal

[3] Nandor Fodor, *Freud, Jung and Occultism*. New York, University Books 1971.

interchanges, but of early pre-natal. The pastoral team tends to become the placenta with a cord firmly attached to the congregational foetus. The 'primary task' of the pastoral team becomes its total task, namely, the care of the 'flock'. Any hints about his or their responding to the Apostolic task of the Church, by going out into highways and bringing in strangers (to share the already limited 'cake'), or proclaiming Christ's good news to the unreached all around, are deeply resented as deviations from the primary pastoral/placental task. That the pastoral team should feel themselves regarded as mere purveyors of services, not as persons, is implicit in this regression.

If these diagnoses have any basis in the real situation, we are in the presence of a *recession* that is actual, now complicated by a *regression* which is metaphorical. This means that the responses people make derive, not from their reasoned and emotionally flexible adult functions, but from the imposition, on a hard life, of metaphors from primitive, pre-rational levels and therefore the responses that are made are also primitive, de-skilled and maladjusted. These metaphors, or images of what is going on, are derived from the deeply stored record of pre-natal, pre-personal conflicts. So the defensive or offensive retaliation is at foetal level. It is inevitably impersonal, and can be inhuman and damaging. At that level there are only *my needs*, and a set of tubes to connect me to where I insist that they still be met.

These are the kinds of situations where people intuitively use metaphors of the 'tight corner' sort. The task of the counsellor is to be able to function well in tight corners. By counsellor I mean to include all the varieties of helping person, professional and lay, whole-time and employed or part-time and voluntary.

For myself, the metaphor 'tight corners' evokes an invigorating, exhilarating prospect of 'getting through a tough spot'. It evokes memories of a birth in which I fought with fierce determination to win through. What obstructs me when going round 'tight corners' or while being 'driven round the bend', is there to be pushed out of the way. Left to myself that is how I handle opposition, so that persons in my way could feel dealt with as if they were things. But I am not 'left to myself'. The monitoring Spirit most characteristically represents the interests of the people who could be the victims of my rough-riding tactics when in 'tight corners'. The here and now of a 'tight' situation, with actual and inescapable elements of strain, constriction and compression, and with some hazards to be feared in negotiating the narrows, need not evoke regressive behaviour, similar though the patterns are.

To an extent that it is difficult for those in professions and trades with a standard practice to realize, those who are in the helping professions are divided by metaphor. The images of the healer's appropriate action in relation to mental pain are often contradictory. The kind of close questioning and listening for signs of the illness, deeper than are easily able to be expressed, which would be felt appropriate in physical medicine, can be scorned as 'morbid curiosity' or 'dangerous probing'. The critical metaphors are loaded with disapproval.

The metaphors of cure in the medicine for sick minds in the Middle Ages, based on the humours, led to interventions producing vomiting, to get the badness out (hence the root of the emetic, Hellebore, became the sign of the physician for the insane) or purging it away, or blood-letting to get rid of the bad humours. In the seventeenth and eighteenth centuries and on into the nineteenth, opium as laudanum was widely prescribed and recommended by patients (such as S. T. Coleridge and William Wilberforce) to each other for 'hypochondriacal' symptoms we would now associate with distress of the foetus in the womb of a distressed mother. The tranquillizing, putting to sleep, 'drugging the pain', metaphor came indeed to Christ in his agony, as a soldier put a sponge of an anodyne to his lips. He tasted it but quietly turned away the relief to which the metaphor of that compassionate act invited him.

The Cross of Christ is the supreme metaphor of the freely chosen suffering of a 'holy righteous man' engaged in the task of reaching those who are 'fast bound in misery and iron'. 'In all their affliction he is afflicted.'

So we turn to examine the alternative metaphors and the quite different perspectives and methods as they present themselves in pastoral and psychiatric practice.

CHAPTER 1

Alternatives in Pastoral Counselling

There is a sharp divide between alternative perspectives and methodologies in both psychiatry and pastoral work. Both these disciplines concern us in the practice of a 'clinical theology'. In practice, psychiatry is either about tranquillization, or discrimination. Tranquillization assumes that the task of the professional is to evaluate pain negatively, in fact to devalue it, and as far as possible to abolish it. Discrimination assumes that helping another means distinguishing between overwhelming mental pain which cannot be borne because of lack of ego-strength, and that which, however strong, can be made an occasion for growing, and may even be necessary for growth to take place at all.

This divide does not fall between psychiatry and pastoral psychology, or between theology and secular therapeutic establishments. It is one which is *within* spiritualities and pastoral care disciplines, and *within* psychiatric and pyschotherapeutic practice, even to some extent within the newer therapies. Some of those who now stress the importance of some kind of spirituality find it difficult to acknowledge the importance of the darker depths of a person. They advise the need to set the mind on higher things, and to be absolved from sin without dwelling on the causes of it. Like their counterparts in psychiatry and in some of the apparently more superficial aspects of some new therapies, they seem unprepared to acknowledge what can be learned from the very tight corners of life, and those related tight places in the soul or psyche of man.

Throughout this book, as throughout my work, runs the belief that pain can, and often should, be faced, using the power of the Holy Spirit, who discerns those who have the strength to bear it, and using the wisdom which has been revealed through the work of pastoral and secular counsellors and therapists. Pastoral counsellors, and those who come to them for help, often find themselves in tight corners. By examining some of these situations, I hope to show their origins, and ways of understanding them which can be used to bring about a fuller sense of what it is to be human, and what has been promised to those who are 'in Christ'.

Those who know my previous book *Clinical Theology* will soon realize how far my colleagues and I have been led since it was published in 1966[1]. The next chapter spells out in some detail the deepening knowledge we have found through working with primal pain. My conviction of the importance of peri-natal experiences, and (even earlier) of the life of the foetus in the womb, will become obvious in succeeding chapters. Most of our tight corners can be understood more fully when viewed from this perspective.

Only at the very end of the period in which I was using LSD 25 in the therapy of neuroses and personality disorders, that is, at the end of the sixties, did I invite those who wanted to work at primal depth, using LSD, to come to residential conferences with spouse or friends. I soon found how greatly this group work helped the process, and wished that I had realized that earlier. At the same time the value of Reichian and bio-energetic techniques broke upon us, and we discovered that deeper breathing alone was a sufficient catalyst for primal recapitulation and assimilation. Nothing more 'chemical' than that was necessary, so we stopped using LSD.

The charismata released by the Holy Spirit to those who meet in Christ's name, for their needs and those of the world to be met, include certain forms of the gifts of knowledge, discernment and wisdom. The use of these has led to a new expectation referred to as 'the healing of the memories'. This is best reported by some Roman Catholic writers, such as Scanlan and McNutt; and, among American Episcopalians, Agnes Sanford and Anne White have had influential ministries in Britain.[2] The latter has set up groups with carefully monitored methods and a good deal of caution about untutored proliferation.

What is new requires discernment, and this is nowhere more

[1] F. Lake, *Clinical Theology*. Darton, Longman and Todd 1966.
[2] M. Scanlan, *Inner Healing*. New York, Paulist Press, 1974.
   F. McNutt, *Healing*. Notre Dame, Indiana, Ave Maria Press, 1974.
   A. Sanford, *Healing Gifts of the Spirit*. Arthur James 1966.

necessary than in the way we use some of the insights and techniques of the newer therapies, which have in the main crossed the
Atlantic to Britain from the United States. Our primal work, I
should make plain, was not 'borrowed' from Janov's primal therapy.
Though he has much to contribute, our work in this area developed
much earlier and independently of his. But we have learned dis-
criminatingly from other writers and therapists, old and new, and
I wish to comment on some of these. This may help the reader to
understand some of the allusions I make to their work in later
chapters.

The Epigenetic Principle

The development of the human personality is orderly. It is an
alternation of periods of growth and transitional crises, through
childhood to adolescence, on to adult life and old age. This has
been described most clearly in the work of Erik Erikson.[3] We grow
according to a kind of ground plan, in which the end is in some
sense present in the beginning, and in which the beginning, and
successive stages, clearly influence the end. Birth is simply one of
the earlier transitional crises, although birth itself is not always
simple. Its complications often lay down an altered ground plan for
later life.

Left and Right Hemispheres

The epigenetic principle is concerned with the development of personality, with manual, intellectual and social skills. Language, too,
develops, and the use of language and mental facilities develops
best in a young person where the psychological environment in
particular provides the right opportunities and support. This particular function is recognized now as belonging to the left hemisphere of the brain.

But we also know now that the right hemisphere of the brain has
a specific function. Holistic thinking, imagination, mythological and
archetypal symbolism, and intuition are largely independent of
words, even though we need to use words to communicate such
experiences and inner vision.

[3] E. Erikson, *Childhood and Society*. Penguin Books 1965.

Kierkegaard distinguishes story-telling from formal schooling, with the right-left difference here being implicit. Of the former he writes:

> The whole point is to bring the poetic into touch with their lives in every way, to exercise a power of enchantment, to let a glimpse appear at the most unexpected moment and then vanish . . . so that the child's soul is electrified and feels, as it were, the omnipresence of something poetic, which is indeed precious to him, but which he nevertheless does not approach too closely. . . In this way the intellectual-emotional mobility is constantly nurtured, a continuing attentiveness to what they hear and see, an attentiveness which otherwise has to be produced by external means.[4]

There is antithesis in our religious tradition between the freedom of the Gospel, proceeding from the same functional right-hemispherical base in the personality, and the rigours of the Law. Rules are gateways to a kind of freedom, for without industry and tested success on the intellectual side there is no freedom in later life to enter any profession or skilled occupation. But freedom to develop the eternal aspect of a man's life needs the right side of the brain. For instance, when Jesus, answering the man who said he would follow him but wanted to go home first, said 'No one who puts his hand to the plough and looks back is fit for the kingdom of God' (Luke 9:62), he was expecting him to be in a state of mind where he had an immediate grasp of all the relevant facts, and could act at once on the basis of a sense of vision, the right-hemispherical task. We become blind to this sense of vision when we are caught up in internal argument, circular thinking and the need for intellectual certainty.

The question needs to be asked whether we are innately endowed to develop in a religious and spiritual sense? Is there a potentiality which can suffer from the same sort of rebuff and atrophy as other primarily right-hemispherical functions, such as emotional mobility? It seems that there is. The right hemisphere is in our culture the more often despised of the two sides of the brain. It can suffer in the irreligious family who can only tolerate 'true' stories. The early intrusion of parental pessimism, cynicism and overriding belief

[4] S. Kierkegaard, *Journals and Papers*, tr. H. V. and E. H. Hong, Indiana, Indiana University Press, 1955. (Four Vols)

in 'realism', can blight this whole faculty. An immense potentiality for growth can be damaged at the outset by parental suppression.

In our primal work and in our growth groups, we use guided imaginings and fantasy journeys. We have learned much here from Gestalt Therapy[5] and from the bio-energetic movement with its sensitivity to posture.[6] They help us to get in touch with the very first pre-verbal experiences laid down in a person. We have been able to learn more than was possible some years ago, when our understanding of the pre-verbal range of personality problems was based on a more verbal approach. People are able to see their life situation in a new way, in a flash, with significant detail. In the progressive changes of scene in imaginative work an inner wisdom is revealed. This quality of seeing enables people to decide instantaneously the way in which their confused relationships should be viewed, and how they are free to decide and to act.

Transactional Analysis

Although I gather that Transactional Analysis (TA) has its own way of approaching pre-verbal material, it is basically a verbal approach. It is, in my view, one of the most flexible and useful of the newer therapies. It is able to release people into a sense of competence in understanding how they can improve on the ways they relate to one another, breaking down barriers, and moving towards a proper intimacy and emotional contact within families and among friends.

TA, as many readers may know, postulates that three particular states of mind exist in all people. Thomas Harris describes it thus:

> It is as if in each person there is the same little person as when he was three years old . . . There are also within him his own parents. These are recordings in the brain of actual experience of internal and external events; the most significant of which happened during the first five years of life. There is a third state, different from these two. The first two are called Parent and Child, and the third, Adult.[7]

Through the Adult the little person can begin to tell the dif-

[5] F. S. Perls, *Gestalt Therapy*. New York, Dell, 1951.
[6] A. Lowen, *Bio-energetics*. New York, Coward McCann and Geoghegan, 1975.
[7] T. A. Harris, *I'm OK, You're OK* (Pan Books 1973), pp. 17–18.

ference between life as it was taught and demonstrated to him (Parent), life as he felt it or wished it or fantasied it (Child) and life as he figures it out by himself (Adult).[8]

This system could hardly be so easily grasped if it had not, in parts, sacrificed depth and adequacy in comprehending man, for the sake of brevity and panache, to a certain superficiality, especially on the frontier with ultimate meanings and morals. Theology must guard those. What has it to say about TA?

In TA the Parent can be nurturing, but whenever it has to take sides between Parent and Child, typical TA rhetoric is down on the Parent, often caricaturing and using comic language to decry restriction in general as Parental. Though TA workers know also the need for the truly nurturing Parent to indicate limits and constraints to the growing child, in the heat of the battle TA literature inclines to rebel with the Child/Adolescent somewhat precipitately. Eric Berne, the founder of TA, tends to speak also as if all social constraint, the Communal Parent, is inimical to the human spirit. Thomas Oden has pointed out how 'It is precisely these constraints that are often ultimately friendly to human freedom and in fact necessary for social existence.'[9]

The demotion of the voice of the valid conscience into that of the ogre Parent is a serious shortcoming when TA is viewed as a Christian pastoral resource. The therapeutic experiences of Freud, Reich, Perls, and Berne (all important figures to me with the development of their thinking seen in psychoanalysis, bodywork, Gestalt and TA respectively) so deluged them in the unhappiness which stems from neurotic guilt that they tended to neglect impressive examples of real guilt. In their different ways each of the four developed a therapy which dissolved the super-ego (Freud), freed man from the repressive moral codes and punitive methods of upbringing (Reich), combated parent-ridden behaviour, preventing the 'top-dog' attacking the 'under-dog' (Perls) and got rid of the 'loser' script, asserting that a person is 'OK' (Berne).

Against these four, Herbert Mowrer, for instance, has criticized the moral sloppiness of much American counselling and group work.[10]

[8] Ibid., p. 30.
[9] T. Oden, *Game Free*. New York, Harper and Row, 1974.
[10] O. H. Mowrer, *The Crisis in Psychiatry and Religion*. Princeton, D. van Nostrand, 1961.

He insists that what is required for human health is not permission to sin, but penitence for sin. TA groups overcome the isolation of guilt by a collusion that everything is 'OK'. In many groups belonging to the charismatic renewal movement, the isolation of guilt is overcome by first overcoming the fear that the guilty self will be rejected, and then speaking out in faith that the outcome will be forgiveness. But the important question is: what is accepted and forgiven by the group, be it a TA or a religious group? Is it the 'me, who is trying to do better', or is it, as by God's forgiveness, the 'whole of me, weak as well as strong, mad with rage as well as meek with apologies, the bad me as well as the good'?

Eric Berne[11] had the Franciscan touch. He would not have the truth wrapped up in psychological jargon. It must be for the common man, the simple man, the young and the old, to understand and use. TA has its own deliverance ministry, mundane but magnificently simple. But TA has no message of eternal life in Christ. Only in places where being pleasantly affirmative equals being Christian could it substitute for or be mistaken for the Gospel.

Eclecticism

Each of the major successful methods of therapy and counselling, Lowen's Bio-energetics, Berne's TA, Perl's Gestalt, Jackins' Re-evaluation Counselling,[12] Glasser's Reality Therapy[13] and Janov's Primal Therapy,[14] has begun with a germ of genius, a sudden discovery of a new way of seeing. This has led to an economical and coherent simplification that had been overlooked by others. Each has developed a training programme, an organization, international outreach, and has accredited representatives to operate in its name.

Those of us who came to these therapies in their early days were introduced to their most productive ideas, and have learned to use them discriminately. Our task is to keep close to the client, as Rogerian,[15] or Truax and Carkhuff[16] counselling training has taught

[11] E. Berne, *Games People Play*. Penguin Books 1964.
[12] H. Jackins, *The Human Situation*. Seattle, National Island Publications, 1973.
[13] W. Glasser, *Reality Therapy*. Harper and Row 1965.
[14] A. Janov, *The Primal Scream*. New York, Putnams, 1970.
[15] C. Rogers, *On Becoming a Person*. Constable 1964.
[16] C. B. Truax and R. R. Carkhuff, *Towards Effective Counselling and Psychotherapy*, Chicago, Aldine, 1967.

us to do. Often when we are unsure as to how to proceed in helping a client, one or other of these methods clicks into focus, and we can offer it as a way of working and understanding.

But I have no loyalty to any one of these particular methods, and I have no wish to stretch its applicability to cover the whole range of human problems. Eclecticism is the correct theological stance. I am grateful to them all, particularly for what they have written so clearly.

CHAPTER 2

Counselling in the Presence of Primal Pain

A Deeper Understanding of Affliction

In the years between 1976 and 1980 we have been led to a new and entirely unexpected understanding of the origins of 'affliction'. This is the most severe, most baffling and most intractable of all the forms of mental pain we meet. Apart from schizophrenia, to which it is in some ways related, it is the most destructive to the self in all its aspects. In my *Clinical Theology*[1] the longest chapter, of over three hundred pages, attempted to deal with this condition, the so-called 'schizoid personality disorder'. I examined it in literature, history, psychiatry, theology, philosophy and in the practical details of pastoral counselling. Those who have been transfixed by total anguish of body, mind, spirit and relationships, cannot help resisting the help they request. They are at one level hostile to their own hope of recovery. Their 'death-wish' is always strong.

Until recent years we attributed this affliction mainly to the anguish of the baby who is not bonded to the mother after birth, but is kept waiting in a loneliness which becomes a panic, then a horror, and then, beyond a certain limit, a dreadful splitting, a falling apart and fragmentation of the whole person, body, soul and spirit. We recognized that there were also limits to the amount of pain that could be borne in the actual process of birth. Beyond those limits, the struggle to love and survive suddenly switched over into a struggle to die. The desire then is to be crushed to death, not to survive, but to attain a longed-for oblivion.

If exposure to this intolerable, 'transmarginal' pain had already

[1] F. Lake, *Clinical Theology*. Darton, Longman & Todd, 1966.

driven the individual across the threshold into a longing for death, within the birth process itself, he or she became more vulnerable, more prone to total affliction after the birth.

Maternal Distress Affecting the Foetus

What we did not recognize then, and have become firmly convinced about only as we have been able to pay attention to even earlier sources of pain, is the vulnerability of the foetus to all that is going on in the mother, particularly in the first trimester. Affliction in its worst forms strikes in the first three months after conception. It is not just the matter of whether the mother was pleased or not to discover that she was pregnant. The either-or of that eventuality comes through with recognizable force in many cases of intra-uterine 'recall'. It is remembered either as a shared delight at being wanted, or as a horror at being a socially disastrous mishap. We have been compelled to look earlier.

There are certain clearly distinguishable phases before the mother even knows she is pregnant. The foetus seems to be in some memorable way aware of these. There is the short preliminary stage as the 'blastocyst'. This is often felt to be a good experience of non-attachment, even of unitive and quite 'transcendent' bliss. It belongs to the week or ten days between conception and implantation in the lining of the womb. In the next stage, the umbilical circulation is established, through the cord and the placenta. As this begins to function, the foetus is evidently put into direct contact with all that is being transmitted round the mother's own body as an expression of her own emotional ups and downs. The foetus feels acutely the feelings which are the product of the mother's life situation, for better or worse, and her personal reactions to it. Before she knows that she is pregnant, the foetus knows what sort of a person this is, in whom he or she is fortunate or fated to be.

This intimate connection of mother and foetus is not so surprising. When we are angry or terrified, every cell in our bodies is informed of the emotional emergency. From the tips of the toes that curl up in tension to the hair that 'stands on end', we show and can recognize the signs and symptoms of these strong emotions. Why should this communication exclude the womb? There are strong traditions in Chinese, Indian and Jewish cultures, emphasizing the importance of giving special support to women during pregnancy, to ensure that they can remain tranquil and at peace. They recognize maternal distress as somehow bad for the foetus. Women instinctively believe this to be so if they have good contact with their own bodies. That current psychodynamic theory infers, by the absence of any theory of significant pre-natal conditioning (except for circulating toxins such as alcohol and nicotine), that there is no noticeable difference between spending nine months in the womb of an abundantly happy mother, or forty unloved weeks inside an anxious, distressed, depressed or suicidally despairing woman, is a fact that strikes many mothers of families as ludicrous. 'Of course it matters how the mother feels,' they say. This maternal intuition has so far been without medical support.

The evidence now available shows how severely the foetus can suffer at this early stage of its development. Most adults who have taken this retrospective journey recognize how closely the afflictions of later life, which had driven them to despair or near suicide, are faithful reproductions of crises first encountered in the earliest weeks of their foetal life.

Before birth, the foetus may be seriously damaged if the mother is dependent on alcohol, nicotine or other drugs. It is also damaged by the less readily identifiable changes that transmit to the baby a mother's rejection of a particular pregnancy and of the life growing within her. Any severe maternal distress, whatever its cause, imprints itself on the foetus. These damaging experiences are now accessible to consciousness without undue difficulty.

Making Sense of Syndromes

I am aware that this chapter now moves into a discussion of pregnancy and childbirth, indeed of ante-natal care and obstetrics. All this might seem out of place in a book on 'Tight Corners in Counselling'. I would not enter on this at all (my experience of midwifery being slight and at least forty years old) were it not that, in order to provide accurate empathy, without which counselling is demonstrably ineffective, I have to make sense, to myself and to the counsellee, of some very strange symptoms. Whatever we may make of them, this much becomes certain, they are not due to any organic disease process in the present. What are they due to? What do we make, for instance, of this syndrome, this collection of associated symptoms. The 'solar plexus' region feels tied up in tight knots; the area beneath the sternum feels like an elongated bag full of 'black badness'. It nauseates, but the desire to 'throw up' has to be blocked by a strangulating internal grip on one's own throat. The terror of vomiting bears no relation to the mere inconvenience of its actually happening. When this occurs in conjunction with tense, painful, stiff and hunched-up shoulders and with feelings of overwhelming physical and mental affliction and personal worthlessness, what do we make of it? What is the diagnosis?

To say, as would a physician of the seventeenth or eighteenth century that together these symptoms constitute 'hypochondriasis' if they occur in a man and 'hysteria' in a woman, is mere naming. We do not know what the names mean in terms of events, experiences and processes. We cannot give any cogent or consistent meaning to the collection. But unless we can, the counsellee will experience our reassurance that there is nothing really (meaning 'organically') wrong, as both a failure of diagnosis, since we cannot see or know through into it, and an inability to empathize. We don't seem to understand how *he* feels. He *knows* there is *something* wrong. Whatever we may do as honest doctors, having eliminated organic disease, to assure him or her that there is 'nothing wrong', he stays unconvinced. Or he trusts our authority because of our personality and role, not because he recognizes our perception of some comprehensible cause. The less honest but perhaps more empathetic practitioners invent ingenious explanations and prescribe potions designed to influence what the patient feels needs to be done. 'I need some opening medicine, doctor.'

There is another syndrome gathered round the descriptive 'diagnostic' term: claustrophobia. Frankly, for years as a psychiatrist I did not know what to make of the claustrophobic's common fear of being shut in, not able to get out in time, and at risk of crushing or suffocating. Not until, that is, in a long series of patients treated with LSD 25 as an abreactive agent, we found consistently that the root of this syndrome was the experience of a difficult birth. So much that had been unsatisfactory in my attempts at empathy ('Were you ever shut in a cupboard?' 'Yes, but it doesn't feel like that, I'm much more helpless and scared than I was then') became a simple matter of confirming the usual history of a difficult birth, going over the symptoms in relation to it, and at times arranging to clinch the matter by reliving it in realistic and convincing detail.

In precisely the same way, four years ago, using a much simpler abreactive technique, facilitating the counsellee in making a 'therapeutic regression' in order to recover the sensations, movements, postures, emotions, images and the stifled unutterable utterances of life early in the womb, we stumbled across the 'maternal-foetal distress syndrome' and recognized it as the actual origin of the 'hypochondriacal-hysterical' syndrome I first mentioned. Hence my otherwise inexplicable interest, as a counsellor of adults, in what was happening to their mothers to distress them in the first third of the pregnancy that produced them, or whether any miscarriage threatened in the middle trimester, or any hazards were identified during the three months preceding the birth.

Traumatic Births

Obstetricians have never doubted that women suffer, and have been dedicated to the relief of that suffering. However, there has been and still is an obstetrical myth that the baby feels nothing of this pain. In spite of the noise of its screaming as soon as it is born, in a way which only a few months later we would confidently assert showed the baby was in pain, obstetricians have maintained that the baby does not feel pain. The enkephalin and endomorphin that are liberated when birth is due undoubtedly diminish pain. Judging from the experience of those who are reliving their births, the fear of crushing and asphyxiation is not removed.

Our now common task of helping people to retrieve repressed experiences to do with their birth, leaves us in no doubt that fear and pain are often experienced, and at once split off from consciousness. The 'emergency' was dissociated and prevented by various gating processes from re-entry into full, contextualized awareness. Those who are, in this way, able to remember events, before, during, and after birth, recall with specific accuracy the bodily sensations, the accompanying emotions, and a detailed sense of the environmental pressures or deficiencies, with a vividness which has etched them for ever on the recording cells of the organism.

So, although for most people the process of birth may be tough but tolerable, for some it can be devastating in its destructiveness. Cataclysmic muscular convulsions turn a peaceful haven into a crushing hell. This 'no-exit' phase, before the cervix begins to open, can last for some hours. The next phase, of travel through the pelvis, is at best an energetic struggle, at worst a brain-destroying, suffocating, twisting, tearing, crushing torture, in which the will to live may be extinguished and a longing to die take its place. The hazards of obstruction, impaction, prolonged delays due to uterine inertia, or sudden violent extrusion when induction puts the uterine muscle in spasm, the hazards of forceps delivery, abnormal presentations, asphyxia as a result of the cord being round the neck, breech births or emergency Caesarean sections, all these possibilities of profound discouragement and catastrophe may occur during this phase. The will to live has often turned here into a desperate desire to die. The baby arrives under brilliant lights, with loud noises, to be gripped by hands that may suspend it by the feet, at times slap it and cut the still-pulsating cord. Then, omitting the whole agenda of the tension-relieving touch of the mother, needed to give a sense of bondedness and reassurance to the infant that both it and the mother have survived the perilous process, omitting all this, the baby is put at some distance away from the mother, to be cot-nursed among other of its unhappy kind, also screaming their protest.

Here the baby may suffer alone the dreadful, unfamiliar enormities of space, unbounded by the expected human hands and face. The newborn may be left alone long enough to be nudged to the edge of the abyss of non-being, trembling through the phase of separation-anxiety, eventually to fall, in a moment of horror, over the edge into nothingness, into the abandonment of hope, love, desire for life and expectation of access to humanity. To add to this legacy of terror, within the next few months, the infant may experience intense hunger, severe cold and hypothermia, love starvation and even baby-battering and child abuse.

These facts are amply brought out by recall of primal experiences, and subsequently confirmed. Some of these damaging factors are on the increase. There are grounds for questioning the wisdom of the obstetrical practice of induction if there is no better reason than to bring more births within convenient working hours.

These peri-natal experiences are powerfully determinative of the whole of a person's background of feeling and attitude to transition or change. It is from these experiences that our perception of the cosmos derives. Our basic expectations of what it means to live *outside* in 'God's world', and to depend on others for gentle handling, love and mercy, take their origin here.

The objection may be raised that, whereas it can be demonstrated objectively that births can be traumatic and infants be neglected, isolated and battered in the earliest months, it can surely not be possible for them to experience such pain and terror during their births, or, if they do, to remember it all later on in life. There is, however, sufficient evidence that peri-natal injuries do lie at the roots of certain personality disorders and irrational fears, sufficient to make this a reputable psychodynamic development. W. D. Winnicott, one of the most highly regarded British paediatricians and psychoanalysts, held the same views about birth and the relevance of birth trauma as I have been outlining. Psychiatrists who value his work in all other respects tend to overlook his papers on birth trauma.[2]

To go back earlier, Otto Rank, one of the original group of psychoanalysts, wrote about it fully in 1923. Freud wrote of Rank's book *The Trauma of Birth*,[3] 'It is the most important progress since the discovery of psychoanalysis.' For personal reasons Freud decided to allow Rank's theory to 'fall flat', but it remains as important a stage in psychodynamic understanding of the archaeology of the self as Freud first said it was. Following Rank, Nandor Fodor, a psychoanalyst of repute, wrote a book on the birth trauma[4] and a second, *Freud, Jung and Occultism*,[5] in which he speaks of the personal reasons why neither Freud nor Jung could accept the theory Rank had so convincingly put forward. As therapy it was bound to fall short of expectation until the pre-natal distresses and their effects had been taken into account.

Numerous psychiatrists, in the days when LSD was used in psycholytic therapy, reported the reliving of birth traumata and of its therapeutic value in claustrophobic reactions. Stanislav Grof,[6] for instance, began work with LSD 25 in 1956, two years after I did. We both recorded relivings of birth and peri-natal events from the earliest days, though for the first three years I resisted my patients' conviction that this was an actual reliving of their birth. Since those days a large number of primal therapists have arisen. The best known and most prolific of them is Arthur Janov. His later book, *The Primal Man*,[7] written in collaboration with a neuro-

[2] D. Winnicott, *Collected Papers*. Tavistock Publications, 1958.
[3] O. Rank, *The Trauma of Birth*. New York, Harper Torch Books, 1934.
[4] N. Fodor, *The Search for the Beloved*. New York, University Books, 1949.
[5] N. Fodor, *Freud, Jung and Occultism*. New York, University Press, 1971.
[6] Stanislav Grof, *Realms of the Human Unconscious*. New York, Viking Press, 1975.
[7] A. Janov and M. Holden, *The Primal Man*. New York, Thos. Cromwell, 1975.

physiologist, Michael Holden, gives extensive information about the reliving of birth trauma.

Distress in the Womb

Although there was ample earlier evidence in the work of Fodor, Peerbolte and F. J. Mott,[8] we had not realized until 1976 how severely painful and how well remembered is the much earlier invasion of the foetus by maternal distress. Nor had we then collected enough 'evidence' to establish the correlation between the origins of this widespread and crippling syndrome of affliction, and the very early and overwhelming invasion of the foetus by maternal anxiety, depression, hatred, despair, coveting, envy, jealousy, and the whole gamut of her bad feelings. Whether these are the consequences of her own bad life situation during the pregnancy, or of a difficult situation now made much worse by her own early conditioning, when she was in *her* mother's womb and in her subsequent childhood, they are, by some mechanism we do not understand, made vividly present to the foetus and become part, the earliest part, of the conditioning or learning process.

There are two elements here. One is the invasion of the foetus by the mother's often complex emotions. She may have been full of anger internally, while fear, compliance or compassion prevented its ever being shown externally. She may have loved the man by whom she became pregnant, while hating the resultant foetus, or loved the prospect of having a baby, while hating, fearing or feeling deeply disappointed and neglected by its father. The foetus receives all such messages, but has difficulty (in so far as primal work provides us with usable evidence on these matters) in distinguishing what relates specifically to it and what belongs to the mother's feelings about her own life in general.

The second element is the foetal response, either to 'take it all to heart' as a judgement against itself, to be passively endured, or strongly to oppose it, or 'to get right out of it' by splitting off the ego, the experiencing 'I' taking leave of the too-badly hurt foetal body.

The tendency is to feel identified with all of these invading maternal emotions in turn and to react to each. This produces, in some

[8] F. J. Mott, *The Universal Design of Creation*. Mark Beech, 1965.

people, a lifelong imprinting of distressful feelings that have nothing whatever to do with any of their own life situations. They prove to be a direct transcript, often in extraordinary and specific detail, of the pregnant mother's disturbance. This may only have been temporary, but was at the time sufficiently impressive, more lastingly so upon the foetus than the mother herself. This imprinting is recognizable in later life in a bewildering variety of ways. It often comes through as a perpetually inappropriate and unwelcome emotional colouring to life.

Predestined to Bear Another's Grief

Let me give an example. An intelligent, handsome and highly talented man had no reason at all to feel a sort of grey sadness pervading everything, coming at him from the walls of his home or office, reflecting back from groups that he could otherwise have enjoyed. His actual life situation, happily married and professionally successful, 'could hardly be better'. It warranted bright colours and good feelings. But a bitter sadness and angry resentment, that felt to be both foreign to him and yet in another sense all too familiar, invaded his person in a way he could not prevent. He felt he was not understood nor attended to, yet he was. He felt himself to be where he did not want to be; but that was nonsense; he was.

On inquiry we discovered that his mother, when carrying him in the womb, had felt exactly this way about her own life. Two years before his birth his parents had escaped from a Russian-occupied country, leaving everything behind save life itself. The father was thankful to have escaped Siberia, and did not agree with his wife's unremitting grief, resentment and refusal to take up life in the new country. He was out of sympathy with her bitter nostalgia. Even thirty years later her deepest longings were still back in the homeland of her youth.

As we discerned the uncanny parallels between his lifelong intrusion-feelings and his mother's well-recorded emotional distress while carrying him, he already began to feel that these emotions were in fact not in any realistic way related to his own life-experience. They belonged to his mother, not to him. He began to want to put them back where they belonged.

When he took his turn to simulate life in the womb and had given his memory free rein to reconstruct his life as a foetus, he began to weep bitterly, feeling helplessly invaded by an intense grief. For two hours he was reliving his all-or-nothing, primal re-actions to this most painful intrusion of maternal distress. At times he wept pitifully, praying for a change to kinder feelings. At times he growled and thrust it away in anger, but that was shortlived. He went into such pain that his cries rose to a long, high-pitched moan. At other times he fought it all, by virtue of a strength learned before the umbilical circulation had been established; but then, after keep-ing this up for what seemed to him like weeks, the prolonged pain overwhelmed him.

He became aware, as he had not been during the history-taking, of his mother's sorrow and concern that his brother, four years older, was difficult, perpetually angry and hostile. He felt her sorrow at not having her mother in the country of exile. Throughout he was eagerly recognizing, one after another, the all-too-familiar emotions and colourings that had dogged him throughout his life. He recognized, beyond any doubt in his own mind (and since we do not, in this exercise, either introduce or interpret these data, he had only his own mind to make up), that the bulk of those bad feelings were not his own at all. They were his mother's defeated response to *her* life situation. Like his father, he was immensely courageous and thankful for life as it came. What he recognized as his own feelings were 'grief at being predestined to be the bearer of griefs that were not his own'. This, to my mind, brought him close to Christ, who willingly took on just such a destiny.

The Roots of the Major Personality Disorders

So whereas we used to attribute the origins of affliction to post-natal dereliction, we now see that to be just one of the roots. The tap root, as it were, which is responsible for many of the most characteristic and severely self-damaging features of schizoid afflic-tion, must now be firmly placed in the first trimester, within three or so months of conception.

It is this intra-uterine period that has consequently become of vital importance to pastoral understanding and counselling. It pro-ceeds from conception and the blastocystic phase, through implan-tation, to the crucial weeks of the first trimester, during which the foetal circulation is established at the end of the fourth week. 'Or-ganogenesis', the essential formation of all bodily organs, is complete by the eleventh week. These first three months produce a complex variety of common syndromes, or symptom-patterns.

All the common diagnostic entities of psychiatric practice, hysterical, depressive, phobic, obsessional, schizoid and paranoid, have their clearly discernible roots in this first trimester. Each of them constitutes a particular view of the foetal-placental world and what goes on in it. We are able to follow what happens when the interchange of satisfactory maternal-foetal emotion, so reliably good as to be scarcely noticed, is interrupted by the influx of maternal distress. How is the badness of this invasive evil dealt with? What happens to the good that was and is still, from time to time, available? What kind of distorted cosmos does this produce? It is important to recognize these 'world views', since they are the same fixated patterns of perception which impose themselves, more mistakenly than accurately, on roughly similar events throughout life.

The archaeology of the self revealed by these studies has its foundations at the beginning of the history of the organism. This leads to an approach which is in sharp contrast to current psychoanalytical method, which tends to begin with contemporary problems. It then moves gradually back in time to adolescence, to childhood, to oedipal problems, and to pre-oedipal conflicts, eventually coming to a halt at birth, which may be excluded as irrelevant or included as significant.

The Integrative Process

What therefore, we propose, to one who suffers, for instance, from an hysterical personality disorder, or anxiety state in which the terrors of being unrecognized or being left alone, or being rejected as worthless, or being basically bad are rampant, is that we first establish together a competent enough 'Adult'. We seek a 'therapeutic alliance' with an Adult, not a Parent-Child transference. We build up the Adult whose task (and not ours) it will be to descend into, identify with, and *give recognition and acceptance to their own inner child of the past and foetus in the womb.* The trust we engender is of this kind. It differs radically from the transference. The person does not discover his Child by projecting the Parent onto a therapist who then 'analyses the transference'. We facilitate his direct access to his own foetal feelings, at the time when he was in direct contact with the mother's personality, and through her with the father's and that of their world beyond.

Connecting and Contextualizing

Each person picks up the sensations and movements which belong to their primal experience. As deep breathing provides the oxygen that facilitates both connecting and discriminating, and as a sober confidence in the group-assisted process grows, these are contextualized in their original time and place. The associated images of the self are connected to the 'scripts' or summaries of experience and reaction, and these again to the associated emotions. In this way the four main tape-recorders of past experience, associated with the left (thinking and reasoning) and right (intuiting and symbolizing) brain hemispheres, the limbic system (emotions) and the brain stem (sensations and movements), which had been gated off from each other in the primal dissociation, are brought together again.

The core injury to trust in, for instance, certain hysterical personalities has to do with the threat of nothingness, non-being, or dread, when recognition has not been given, attention too long delayed, when absence has been too cruel to be borne or dereliction so dreadful that life was despaired of and death hoped for. It is in order that the person can bear these foetal and babyhood experiences in full consciousness that we and all his other resources, human and godly, are strengthening him. The task is no longer difficult to discern. The achievement of a full integration depends on a variety of dynamic factors. There is no one 'action handle' but many. Our task is to be aware of the significant ones and to turn them.

Stitching

A metaphor we find useful is that of 'stitching'. In foetal life and later, the seam of the cloth of selfhood was over-stretched, then torn under the distress and pain of maternal-foetal or 'umbilical' penetration, or of birth, and then of post-natal injuries to trust. The weak, hurt, humiliated, fearful and now also feared and hated self, is that part of the cloth that falls down into the actively repressed and dissociated 'unconscious'. The conscious self pulls up and away, in fear and disgust, in disapproval and scorn of the weak self. It resolves to be strong and stay always strong, out of contact with any vestiges of the old despised weakness. So the human race lives, in flight from those forgotten truths, anxious to maintain the façade of competence and mastery. This is an extravagant waste of energy, spent on denial, on continuous repression, and on a host of hectic activities serving no other purpose than to reassure the fugitive that the pursuers can never catch up, that failure of the defences will never happen, that contact will never again be made with the vulnerabilities with which we all began, and that guile is the way to gain.

Dismantling the Defences: the Strategy of Integration

Those who self-select themselves to come on these 'Workshops' for five or six days, living and working together with others of the same mind, have already set in motion a contrary strategy. They intend to 'stitch up' the torn garment of the self, using the enhanced strength, understanding and support of their 'Adult' to reach down to the hurt 'Child', identify with it, suffer with it, give it a voice, and bring it, by empathy, respect and genuine care, fully into contact with the Adult self and the good selves of the surrounding friends. The torn garment of the self is thus 'stitched' into wholeness again.

The rhythm† is that of a deeper than usual breathing. 'Breathe, up into your strength. Wait . . . Now down into your weakness' (or whatever else emerges of primal joy or grief). 'Wait . . . Now up again . . .' This is the fourfold rhythm or dynamic cycle which is the physiological basis to the reintegrative task.

The procedure at our Primal Integration Conferences or Workshops is first to take an accurate history of the trouble. This is a cognitive, intellectual task. But the memory of events at such a depth is pre-verbal. Sometimes we reach down to these memories by focusing on the spontaneous images produced by the right hemisphere. A journey in the imagination to some cave deep in the sea takes the recumbent person into a readiness to pick up these primal images. Nowadays we more usually open up on conception and post-conception 'memories' by inviting the subjects to feel into their mother's and father's feelings about themselves, their relationship and their general life situation on the evening of the conception.

They are often astonished at how vividly and movingly they can reconstruct the relationship within which they were conceived.

Thus they reach down into long-lost emotions, which could in no way be *expressed* during intra-uterine life, and which (and this is vital to successful coping) could in no way be shared with anyone so long as the mother was being felt as the 'attacker'. With the breathing-out, we invite the person to give vent to the sound which is suggested by the emotion he is getting in contact with. These deep origins of affliction give rise to some heart-breaking, tormented and convincing sounds of anguish. The work we set out to do can therefore be seen as the connection and reconciliation of four essential aspects of experience: the cognition, the imagination, the sensation and the emotion. Primal pain has split them apart. We aim to help the recognition of them all in their original uterine context.

It is a striking fact that four subjects can be working in the same large room, each curled up in the foetal position on a mattress on the floor, each with a facilitator from the house staff or other conference member, a scribe to take verbatim notes and a third who may supervise a tape recording. After the initial introduction, the subject will be almost totally unaware of and unaffected by the others outside his own small group. They genuinely create 'a womb' out of the small group and experience within it an authentic transcript of intra-uterine experience. I rehearse, in a neutral, rather 'dead-pan' voice, the well-known anatomico-physiological facts from conception, through implantation to the establishment of the umbilical circulation. Each makes his spontaneous response at each stage. This is both written down and tape-recorded. I usually then leave each group to take their own time to proceed through the three trimesters and on through birth until breathing and bonding have been established. At four-or-five weeks, at the moment when three fingers of the facilitator are placed over the subject's navel symbolically to indicate the establishment of the foetal-placental circulation, he is invited to breathe up fully and then breathe out, expressing, by a change in the neutral expiratory noise, the prenatal emotion they feel to be reaching down to at depth. At that moment, or within a few minutes, it is usual to hear as many distinct and totally different responses as there are subjects working in the same large room.

One will be expressing deep joy, rarely the delectable (or detestable) participation in the mother's bodily experience of sexual intercourse, another enjoying a quiet peacefulness. Another will be feeling a strange longing for recognition, first, perhaps, that the mother should recognize and be in touch with her own body. Often she is not, and is too busy to be so. The foetus needs to know that the mother recognizes its being there and is glad of it. This, too, is often not the case. One will be trembling in fear at the absence of recognition and powerfully yearning for it. Another will be plunged into strong crying and tears, weeping, we may learn later, with the mother's weeping for a dying parent. We hear the mother's bitter crying, which she may herself have suppressed, coming out in the foetus twenty or forty years later.

Quite astonishing is the non-intrusiveness to others of those who go down into such appalling invasion by maternal distress that they cry out loudly, groan and even scream or shout their anguish and anger at the pain and frustration of it. Yet each is separate, helped by the sense that others are working, yet authentically in their own 'womb space'. They remain specifically concentrated on their own reliving. This provides an element of control which gives more credence to the result as a genuine personal recall, not influenced by me or by what others are recalling.

In contrast to the therapies that propose some alleviation of the primal dread of non-being, or that offer some escape of the self from a suffering that has been depersonalized into mere aches, we recognize that *the symptoms we complain of are the only language the small, foetal person has available with which to draw our adult attention to its injured and trapped presence within us*. We do not run away from cries for help from babies and children. Or do we? This therapeutic journey is to hear, go to, be with, and within, to feel with and help that small person to bear and express that pain. Being encouraged to do this, and finding it shared with love, casts out the fear of it. The terrified child from which the adult had been in flight, feels itself calmed and cared for.

Time, Place and Person

Christianly speaking, the way of escape is *not by some supernatural relief* of the symptoms, an offer of peace as the world gives peace. This would not be peace but only a tranquillized state. Christ has provided a *supernatural use of affliction*, by making it the deepest and most costly place of his presence, alongside and within the humanity he made. In redemptive identification he has reached down to precisely when and where we were and are most lost. So the care and cure of foetal insignificance, and loneliness, or the bewildered dereliction of babyhood, consist in retracing our steps to the time and place of the original catastrophic loss in which the whole primitive person was split or fragmented. What could not be borne then, can be assimilated, reconciled and borne, without again splitting now.

Such sufferers have often heard themselves saying, on some fine morning, 'I'm in a dreadful place. I can't stand it.' The time has *seemed* to be the present, so powerful is the resonance from primal catastrophes. The effect of this reintegrative journey is to retrace our steps until the time *and place* of all that has been so troublesome for so long are clearly and unmistakably identified and not evaded. On this occasion all the split-off bits of the self, the thinking and talking, imaging or picturing, feeling, grieving or fearing, are connected up in the reliving of it all, *the time and place known for the first time in their true context*. It is this truth that frees. It is part of the work of Christ to make that truth tolerable. Indeed his Cross could be said to be raising the perpetual question, 'Must you not go deeper to seek the sources of your discord and despair? Can any meeting place less deep, less hidden, less threatening than this be the place where the rooted resistances of human beings to loving and living, to health and holiness are to be reached and reconciled?'

Three-branched Affliction Rooted in the Stricken Tree

Reading again the brilliantly perceptive work of Simone Weil on affliction, there are passages and metaphors which speak directly into the life of the distressed foetus in the first trimester, but not at all into the circumstances and experiences, images and context of post-natal affliction. These passages from *Gateway to God* [9] are good examples:

If the tree of life, and not simply the divine seed, is already formed in a man's soul at the time when extreme affliction strikes him, then he is nailed to the same cross as Christ.

[I would take the 'divine seed' to be the experience of blastocystic bliss and the 'tree of life' to be the establishment of the

[9] S. Weil, *Gateway to God* (Fontana, 1974). p. 87.

umbilical circulation. It is certainly true that affliction experienced at this stage, in total innocence, partakes of the suffering of the Lamb of God.]

Everyone feels the existence of evil and feels horror at it and wants to get free from it. Evil is neither suffering nor sin; it is both at the same time, it is something common to them both. For they are linked together; sin makes us suffer and suffering makes us evil, and this indissoluble complex of suffering and sin is the evil in which we are submerged against our will, and to our horror.

A part of the evil that is within us we project into the objects of our attention and desire; and they reflect it back to us, as if the evil came from them. It is for this reason that any place where we find ourselves submerged in evil inspires us with hatred and disgust. It seems to us that the place itself is imprisoning us in evil. Thus an invalid comes to hate his room and the people around him, even if they are dear to him, and workers sometimes hate their factory, and so on.

Simone Weil's searching analysis of affliction[10] corresponds to the psychiatric diagnosis of the schizoid *position* (that abyss from which the schizoid personality *defences* are in flight). This French philosopher, mystic and revolutionary describes it as a threefold pain, made up of a social scorn, a splitting mental pain and bodily anguish. I would say, with no fear of being wrong, that *this tripartite terror is a direct result of transmarginal distress in the foetus, usually within the first trimester.* (Occasionally, an accidental near-miscarriage or attempted abortion in the third or fourth month can produce some of this affliction, as can a long and cruelly difficult labour.)

I will now summarize the schizoid position as it reveals itself to us in the affliction of early intra-uterine life.

The Social Scorn

There is a sense of being pierced by a 'nail' of affliction. It pierces a live body through its middle. It is variously described as a 'poisoned screw', a 'spear', an 'iron rod', a 'thorn-covered twig' or, a 'cork-screw'. If the invasion is displaced, the patient feels he or she is, like Job, being pierced all over with stinging arrows, or needled

[10] S. Weil, *Waiting on God*. Fontana, 1959.

or goaded. The total lack of recognition leads the foetus to feel degraded, less than human, turned to stone or dust, bad, black, inanimate, sub-human. This often has several components, such as the social scorn which may be the unmarried mother's lot, her disgust at her own reproductive organs, and her hatred of this pregnancy and its product. These lead directly to self-scorn, self-hatred and self-horror. Revulsion is turned inward. There is most commonly *a profound and permanent sense of worthlessness.* 'If my presence in my own mother aroused no sense at all of worth, in spite of such longing, must I not accept that verdict of condemnation for ever?' Such people feel orphans, disinherited, with no family, no stake in the past or foot-hold on the future. They feel a profound guilt, which Simone Weil says we could understand in criminals. But *they* do not feel it; it is the innocent who do, in proportion to their innocence. It is not so much guilt for having done wrong, but rather, it is a guilt of existing at all, a remorse at being a self. God is felt to be infinitely distant and disinterested when he is not condemning, and condemnatory when he comes close.

The Mental Pain

There is, when people undergo transmarginal splitting during the reliving of foetal life, a sense of being torn apart. This can be 'molar', whole masses of the body being split off and surrendered to the black and evil flood, such as the part of the body below the waist, or the diaphragm or neck; or the left side can be surrendered as 'sinister' and the right side 'rightly' barricaded off from it in a defensive 'goodness'. A typical picture, confirmed by the spontaneous art of many afflicted persons, is that of the 'good' embryo taking refuge in the foetal skull, to escape from the black flood. If even this is invaded, the self can, with a violent burst of energy, 'escape' through the centre of the brow or the top of the head. It is then quite outside the body, which is left as an existence without energy or spirit, an empty hulk. The total detachment of the ego is a real possibility in affliction. All this occurs in the first trimester.

The splitting can be, not 'molar' but 'molecular', that is, not a splitting of a tree-trunk into large chunks, but rather a fragmentation, as of a shattered stone. This is experienced as a disintegration of the self, a valley of scattered dry bones. The self feels unreal, not personal but 'all in bits'.

The Physical Anguish: Placement and Displacement

It is an inexplicable fact that, during the reliving of foetal distress of this sort from the first trimester, there is commonly experienced a severe pain at the navel or near it. At times it is higher, over the solar plexus, but rarely lower. The skin round the navel is often sore and a local dermatitis is quite common, both during the recall and in the person's history, at times of tension. An irrational fear of pollution getting in at the navel has prevented people from taking a bath while the eczema lasts. The local invasion point is often in agonizing pain, with the emotional distress of the mother seeming to focus at that point.‡ I do not pretend to understand how that comes about. From the point of entry the black and bitter flood (the colour and texture of it are variously described, mostly in unpleasant terms such as lumpy, hard, oily, dirty, black, brown, or green and bitter or shitty) spreads out into the body. Attempts are made to stem the flood but *these are symbolic, not primarily physiological*, though they become secondarily so, as the body begins to react as if in an allergic rejection. We have shown how, in addition to a general sense of wretchedness, malaise (weakening, defilement or poisoning), there are displacements which lead directly to bodily symptoms, nausea, retching, fear of vomiting rather than actual vomiting, coughing and spitting, 'nervous diarrhoea' or colitis, irritable bowel or bladder, frequency of urination, and the like.

Displacement of 'negative umbilical affect' takes place, as Francis Mott showed, into any structures which can demonstrate a relationship of a nucleus to a periphery, of such a kind that activity, such as squeezing, in the outer or peripheral organ can push the contained nuclear material, along it and away, to be 'got rid of'. Bowel movements can push the badness away from the vulnerable belly down to the rectum, or, by reversed peristalsis, up to the throat. Muscles round a joint that is nominated symbolically to carry the badness go into spasm. They contract to confine it and 'kill it off', treating it exactly as if it were a 'foreign body'. The 'bitter blackness' (what the physicians of an earlier generation called 'atrabilious humours' or the 'black bile' of 'melancholy', and saw as the source of hypochondriasis in men and hysteria in women)* can be pushed down the legs to the feet, the skin of which is then fiercely attacked and torn off, and the joints flexed into a painful, 'claw'.

'Looks could Kill'

What is analogous, but at first surprised me, is the displacement of negative umbilical affect into the eyes. The patient feels that the badness and worthlessness that was put there, long before the eyes were used for seeing, is visible to all. They turn their eyes away so as not to be looked at, or what is feared, looked into. Switching from an inhibiting, passive mode to an excitatory, active one, there is also a real fear that such evil looks could kill. One way and another, eye-to-eye contact is difficult for the afflicted to achieve. It can be the very hardest thing for them to do.

The Skin as Indicator

Displacement into the skin is effected when the foetus identifies with the 'shameful badness' of itself, then in the womb, despised and only fit to be scorned. At the same time, to put the badness in the skin keeps it away from the central core of the self and its organs. Such persons are often born with, or soon fall victim to, atopic eczema and may be troubled with skin rashes for a life time or part of it.

By contrast, the 'hysterical' personality tends to keep the skin as good, attractive, fresh and 'deceptively' young looking, with their clothes and personality to match. Unhappily this means retaining the badness of the influx from the distressed or angry mother in the person's own internal organs. They feel that the inner abdominal organs, at times the heart and lungs, but most often the uterus and pelvis, have been destined and given over to badness. Woe betide the foetus whose lot is to spend its first forty weeks in such a desolate and deadly place.

This is not the place to study in detail the origins, in 'negative umbilical affect' and the maternal-foetus distress syndrome, of the main personality disorders, depressive, hysterical, schizoid, paranoid, phobic, obsessional and psychopathic. (Chapter 9 does, however, take up the relevance of this hypothesis in the counselling of the young violent offender, who provides a real tight corner for his or her counsellor.)

The Roots of Pyschosomatic Stress

There is evidence that it is here that we must look for the origins of the major psychosomatic disorders. Wherever a whole embryonic tissue is affected, such as chronic inflammation of mesodermal structures all over the body, in rheumatic and polymyalgia conditions, or widely distributed in endodermal or ectodermal structures, the point of application of the stress is almost certainly at this embryonic stage.

Primary Shock, Adaptation and Exhaustion

The lungs, while still airless, have plain muscle surrounding bronchial passages that can go into spasm to express this desperate need for displacement, followed at once by a fear-bound inability to do other than strangulate the expressive impulse. Asthma, it seems, has some origins down here, as do all the other allergic conditions. The primary shock, that demands lifelong adaptation to keep away from its recurrence is probably this same intra-uterine shock. This is the more probable since, when, in later life, the adaptation fails in exhaustion, what the patient falls back into is the typical maternal-foetus distress syndrome or some aspect of it.

Comprehension: a Factor in Empathy.

This hypothesis is offered to pastoral and other counsellors because it falls to them to counsel many people who are suffering from 'functional' disorders which, in the course of time, have become organic and chronic. They need to be offered 'accurate empathy' if the counselling is to be effective. If this hypothesis is relevant in a case and is surviving under test, not only will the symptomatology be recognized as drawn from the maternal-foetal distress syndrome, but the family history will show the mother as, for some reason or other, distressed when she had this now distressed adult in her womb.

The ordinary run of counselling will probably not offer the direct reliving of the womb life experience. However, a relevant fantasy journey, or just 'staying with' the present symptoms, imagined as taking place 'in utero', can often produce a sufficiently convincing connection and contextualization to enable the counsellee to reallocate the complained-of feelings. They are recognized as belonging either to the mother, whose they originally were, the suffering victim as she was in her own world, or to the original foetal reactions to that transfused invasive terror.

If this outline of the maternal-foetal distress syndrome serves to alert counsellors to the possibility that the time and place that call out for their accurate empathy, lie, at times, between conception and birth, and enable the hurt foetal self to come to recognition, acceptance, expression and reconciliation, its purpose will have been well served.

† *Deep Breathing and Theta Rhythm:* When in 1969 we followed the Reichian hint and began to rely on deep breathing, with a long, vocalized expiration, to touch off the recall of early 'unconsciously remembered' experiences, we had no idea how this worked, as it certainly does.

In the twelve years that we have used deep breathing, in preference to the LSD we administered for the fifteen years before that, the more natural method has proved superior. LSD acts beyond the conscious control of the subject, sometimes throwing up material he or she is not ready to deal with. By contrast, breathing is a self-regulated act with a built-in control. Also, insofar as pre-natal memories are concerned, under LSD the subject avoids the actual terrors or joys of the foetus itself and evades the recognition that this is happening to them in the context of their own mother's womb. Deep breathing, however, promotes a faithful owning and 'contextualizing' of the intra-uterine experience. Under LSD the actual experience of the individual was removed to the realm of myths and to the dream-like sequences which occur in symbolically stated 'religous' conflicts and deliverances. Stanislav Grof's work, continuing to employ LSD, confirms this observation.

Recent work has shown that the pattern of deep breathing we stumbled on actually produces theta rhythm activity in the brain, and that the deliberate production of theta rhythm is an ideal biofeedback method of reaching down to retrieve the memory of very early experiences that have been stored away in 'the unconscious'. In his book *Toward a Science of Consciousness* (New York, Delta Books, 1978) Kenneth R. Pelletier summarizes this recent work on theta rhythm:

> Thus, theta rhythm appears to be a link between conscious awareness and subconscious imagery and associations; as such, it could become an invaluable means of exploring the deep roots of mental phenomena. These studies indicate that controlled production of theta rhythm activity may be an important technique in the exploration of the phenomenology of consciousness.

> In this interface state, an individual appears to be able to use his conscious mind to focus upon unconscious imagery in a paradoxical manner resembling controlled free association. The ability to focus on unconscious processes allows an individual to formulate more creative problem solutions – taking advantage of previously unavailable information from his subconscious mind.

> One additional finding, regarding respiration patterns, was of significance. Respiration patterns during alpha-dominant states consisted of thoracic activity equal to abdominal activity accompanied by a rhythmic pattern of inhalation equal to exhalation. Theta-dominant respiration patterns consisted of abdominal activity greater than thoracic activity accompanied by short, rapid inhalation and slow prolonged exhalation. These respiration patterns may become

extremely useful in clinical biofeedback practice. Patients may be instructed to use their own respiration patterns as feedback for maintaining alpha or theta dominance.

When these neurophysiological findings are linked with Pribram's work on the holographic, and therefore cellular and not neural basis of long-term memory, the theoretical foundations of this hypothesis are provided independently of the work itself, by an appropriately sophisticated scientific methodology. It is no longer neurophysiologically absurd to postulate a Maternal-Foetal Distress Syndrome, propagated by cell division, so that through the years the memory does not decay, but remains active in all the descendents of the cells that originally suffered, becoming available when a particular pattern of deep breathing stimulates the theta rhythm as probe and messenger.

‡ *Apley's Rule:* In paediatric practice, Apley's rule about functional abdominal pain in children states: 'The further the site of the pain from the umbilicus the more likely it is to be organic'. Since only one in twenty of Apley's series proved to have pain of organic origin, the nineteen whose pain, nearer the navel, was severe enough to warrant admission to hospital, were, by the same rule, of functional origin. The present hypothesis proposes that what is troubling these children, 'the little belly-achers', is, in fact, the persistence or escape from repression of 'negative umbilical affect', part of the maternal-foetal distress syndrome. Since the prognosis is poor, one-third continuing to suffer from pain and a further one-third suffering from other neurotic symptoms, including migraine, many would continue unchanged into adult life. (Apley *The Child with Abdominal Pain.* Blackwell Scientific Publications 1975.)

* Sir Richard Blackmore, physician to William III and Queen Anne wrote a treatise on hypochondriacal and hysterical affections in 1725. He wrote, 'I take them to be the same malady.' Even though it was necessary to contend that these are due to 'a delusive Imagination, yet it must be allowed, that let the Cause of such Symptoms be never so chimerical and fantastick, the consequent Sufferings are without doubt real and unfeigned. Terrible Ideas, formed only in the Imagination, will effect the Brain and Body with painful sensations.' The condition was still referred to as 'the Vapours, from the opinion of the ancient Physicians, who imagined that it consisted in the Elevation of dark Fumes and Exhalations from the Matrice (the womb); which rising up in unwholesome Clouds, produce Sufferings in various Parts of the Body where they used to spread their unhappy Influence. . . .Hence the disease is sometimes called Fits of the Mother, sometimes a Suffocation of the Womb, and sometimes Hysteric Affections. . .Thus as the primitive Doctors before mentioned, imagined that all Hypochondriacal Symptoms were derived from a Collection of black Dregs and Lees separated from the Blood, and lodged in the Spleen; whence, as they supposed, noxious Reeks and cloudy Evaporations were always ascending to the superior Regions (the Chest, the Heart, and Head which by turns were made *the Seat of Hypochondriacal War, turbulent Conflicts, and seditious Insurrections*) to the great Distraction and Confusion of the animal State.'

This is a brilliant summary of the way in which ancient medicine attempted to grapple with the fact of 'negative umbilical affect' and give it the only expression appropriate to it, namely a symbolic one.

In his next sentence Sir Richard Blackmore shows exactly why the ancient theory of humours was abandoned by the medical profession, which could only conceive of things happening in the body on the basis of observable structures. That imagination, symbol and metaphor could provide 'passages' of their own was beyond the scope of their rationalism. He wrote, 'But as there are no Passages, or proper Conveyances, by which these Steams and Exhalations may mount from the inferior to the superior

Parts, besides other insuperable Difficulties that encumber this Opinion, *it is now exploded by learned Men*, though retained, at least in Name, among the People.'

Incidentally Sir Richard gives, in this treatise 'the first reasoned account for and against the prolonged use of 'pacifick Medicine', what now we call 'tranquillizers'. He was firm in his recommendation of opium in controlled doses. Though recognizing the risk of addiction he did not consider it too great. (R. Hunter and I. Macalpine *Three Hundred Years of Psychiatry* (Oxford University Press 1963) p. 319ff.)

CHAPTER 3

The Implications for Counselling of Pre-natal Distress

Some Implications of the Hypothesis that Maternal Conditions Affect the Foetus

This hypothesis emphasizes the importance to foetal development of conditions in the mother affecting the growing person in her womb. Insofar as the hypothesis continues to resist attempts to nullify it, certain theoretical and practical implications inevitably arise. We must expect serious consequences whenever foetal life has been put at risk, from maternal distress, addiction, suicidal attempts, attempts at abortion or threatened miscarriage. We are, as doctors, accustomed to observing, recording and evaluating detectable physical damage and morbidity, but have hardly begun to do the same for emotional morbidity where the personal soul and spirit are at risk. The self can die in a surviving body.

Those consequences will be among the basic data of personality difficulties the counsellor has to deal with. In offering accurate empathy, that is, in drawing alongside the distressed feelings, fearful images, painful symptoms and strange sensations of the counsellee, the helper will be, so to speak, getting inside the womb with them, exploring the vicissitudes of life before birth.

Counselling is not only concerned with the repair of the torn trust of the child now reappearing in troubled adults. These same adults are also often parents or prospective parents. They have a poignant sense of responsibility to their children, born and as yet unborn, not to repeat if possible the same catastrophes of mismanagement. They may be more sensitive to these issues than their attendant physicians and the nurses who advise them about ante-natal preparations.

When young parents decide, on the evidence available to them, to have their next baby born in as 'natural' a way as possible, avoiding induction except for specific emergencies, they, too, could well understand that, in aiming for a quiet and gentle arrival, for early and prolonged bonding and for the presence of the father throughout, to share the experience and sustain his wife, they have to negotiate with doctors and midwives before they can put their convictions into practice, however firmly and cogently they hold them.

That should not be the case with these issues which are now pressing ones for our society, if there is a substantial basis to these findings, and subsequent work confirms them. Any mother and father who read this and have an intuitive sense of its truth can decide, when next a pregnancy test is positive, and even before, if their intention is to have a baby, *to give priority to the provision of a peaceful and harmonious environment for the mother.*

A young couple could decide, on learning that a baby was on the way, to devote half an hour a day to being quiet or singing to it in celebration of the person who was coming to awareness within, to assure him or her, with equal delight, of a joyful welcome. There is firm evidence that music heard *in utero*, associated with a restful, peaceful mother, continues to be recognized and to have the same effect after birth, reproducing in the baby the mother's state of calm.

As to judging whether it is credible that the emotional state of the mother could significantly affect the foetus and make or mar its own emotional development, the evaluation and replication of the work here presented is already going on in several psychiatric hospitals, whose psychiatrists have worked with us, and in the enhanced practice of therapists of various schools who have studied with us and sent their clients. Most of all it is being used in lay and religious communities, mainly those which have been stimulated by Renewal to look deeper into the work of the Holy Spirit both in his office as joy-bearer and as chief-groaner (to construct a title out of Rom 8:26).

Implications for a New Theoretical Model of Personality Origins

I have spent nearly forty-four years as a doctor and twenty-nine as a psychiatrist with some unexamined and quite contradictory assumptions about life in the womb. I thought of it, as many colleagues have done, as a protected, comfortable if not blissful place, in sharp contrast to the turbulent world into which the baby came at birth. Alongside that reassuring picture I had a horrific one. Pre-natal excursions were dangerous, apt to precipitate psychoses, not at all to be entered upon lightly, and advisedly avoided. Nor did it occur to me then that, so far as existing psychodynamic theory goes, there was any significant difference, certainly none that a therapist needs take any account of, between spending the nine months between conception and birth in a happy woman, happy in her home, her husband, her background and a foreground of delight at the prospect of the outcome of the pregnancy, and spending nine months in a miserable creature, in an unstable background with multiple marital troubles if she is married at all, who has seriously considered and maybe even attempted an abortion, who worries her way through life, or greets each day with depressive gloom and despair. Since we had allowed no theory of pre-natal influencing we were left with the assumption that it makes no difference.

When I mention to women, especially married ones who have had children, that this is the present case in psychodynamic theory, they are shocked and even appalled. Their own convictions as to the importance of their own states of mind to the well-being of the foetus they were carrying have been for them always a paramount factor, an axiom of existence during a pregnancy. Many stable cultures have included this special care of the pregnant mother in their traditions. I have a sense that our culture will become increasingly unstable unless we do the same.

Mothers can be encouraged to take as much care to be at peace with themselves in the nine months before the birth as in the nine months of concentrated nursing after it. Their husbands, friends and neighbours can offer to share unavoidable loads to make that possible. For Christians, their radical discipleship and for humanists their care of all things human, could, in the presence of these possibilities opt for a different set of life priorities, to give space to 'womb rupture', the unseen nurturing of the spirit and heart, mind and body of the unborn person.

Implications for Research

I was speaking some time ago to a group which included an American mother of three daughters. She returned to me excitedly a few hours later, saying that what I had said explained for the first time the behaviour of the middle daughter. What made it significant was that a number of other girls in her class were behaving in almost exactly the same way. They had manifested an unaccountable tendency to break down suddenly into crying and sobbing. They were not just sad, but deeply distressed with a cutting sense of shame and guilt that some terrible thing had happened. What it was they were devastated by, or why they did it, neither they nor their parents had any idea. Her elder daughter and her classmates in the form above had no such tendency, nor had the daughter lower down in the school and her friends. They had wondered about an hysterical group phenomenon, but it was most unlike such outbreaks. The illumination that had come to her she expressed by saying, 'I have just realized that that was exactly my behaviour in 1963, when my daughter was early on in my womb, as the other girls would be in their mothers, when J. F. Kennedy was shot. That was exactly my behaviour. For weeks we were prone to breaking into tears, with just those feelings about the shooting of the President. The whole thing makes sense to me for the first time.' I offer that gratis as a subject for research.

Implications of Abortion

It is no longer possible to assume that the foetus up to twenty-four or twenty-eight weeks has no feelings when it is being aborted. Even at four weeks there is a highly developed organism reacting with purposive movement and rudimentary feeling to changes in the environment. By eleven weeks, with the completion of the basic genesis of organs, the foetus, as we know from the reliving of attempted or failed abortions at that time, knows that its presence is resented and its life is in danger. It relives its own near-murder with quite shocking accuracy and overwhelming terror.

Working recently with a senior and successful business executive who had been born in the East End of London, to a mother he adored and had every reason to admire for her courage in great adversity, he came suddenly, after weeks and months of delight at being in the womb of so loving a woman, upon a period of great disturbance in her life, followed by a feeling that he was being poisoned. He was convinced that it was an attempted abortion in which he nearly died, after suffering a long anguish of toxic wretchedness. Then he was astounded to feel his mother feeling guilty, appalled at what she had done, trying to forget it. The rest of the nine months were uneventful, though with an increasing sense of how greatly he was loved.

All his married life, and in his relations with any group that could be said to surround him intimately, he had lived in terror of a sudden and unexpected attack on his life, perhaps by poisoning. This led him to being at times both cruel and unjust, suspicious and wary of those closest to him. This reliving put an end to that fear. He had other things to deal with; all was not suddenly rosy, but at least that disruptive fear was behind him.

Incidentally, he remembered that his mother, in later years, when a neighbour with a very large family shared with her the fact of another pregnancy and her desire to have it aborted, had 'hit the roof', in an intense over-reaction, threatening to report the neighbour to the police should she go ahead with it. At first, he said, that memory inclined him to pooh-pooh the idea that she could herself have attempted an abortion, but on reflection the over-reaction, 'protesting too much', pointed to her own unresolved guilt.

Intra-uterine Circumstances Projected onto Groups

The implications of these findings about the early uterine origin of personality difficulties and the distorted perceptions of relationships which perpetuate them, are not limited to intra-personal effects or even their effects in families. The metaphor persists whatever the size of the organizational unit. Like a pastry cutter, you can imagine the same shape coming in all sizes. Pre-natal and peri-natal events are so deeply imprinted upon the human organism that the uterine life-style imposes itself on all subsequent groups of which the person is a member. The boundaries of his place of work or worship, of his community or nation, or even the earth itself (now more aware of its boundaries than ever before) can be experienced precisely as he or she experienced the boundaries of the womb. If the internal state of the group or institution becomes confused, as in transition it is bound to do, the afflicted (paranoid-hystero-schizoid) person is apt to regress. He or she will then add, to the actual lack of clarity, the whole compendium of his or her intra-uterine confusion and its associated violent emotions.

If, for political and economic reasons, recession bites into a school, reducing all manner of supplies and support, recognition and reward, the teacher with a record of pre-natal deprivation can be plunged into the whole welter of primal feelings of persecutory loss, of placental deficiency, even of despair of survival. To *actual recession* and its effects on the adult is added '*neurotic*' *regression* and all its original effects upon the foetus. Lloyd de Mause, the psycho-historian, says bluntly that 'groups, whether face-to-face or historical, induce a "fetal trance state" in their members, reawakening specific physical memories from uterine and peri-natal life.' 'Man is a political animal, as Aristotle said, because for most civilized people, only life in a group can establish contact with repressed fetal emotions.'[1] This extends our hypothesis of the maternal-foetus distress syndrome into sociology, anthropology, business administration and every kind of leadership and membership of groups. Its dimensions become world-wide and the risk global. Recession is, in many respects, inevitable, and we need clear-headedness and flexibility to adapt to it, making a virtue of necessity. Though recession is inevitable, regression, with its accompaniment of rigidity, immature demands, muddle-headedness and surrender to collective selfishness and short-sighted greed, is not inevitable. The responsibility laid on the leadership of institutions and groups of all sizes, to forestall regression, is increasingly urgent. Failure will be momentous in its effects, for regressed behaviour in the mass is a very ugly thing. Half the battle in forestalling a catastrophe is to foresee it and to have a clear analytical grasp of the factors that are liable to produce it.

So long as institutions were expanding, the models based on post-natal dynamics, from Bion's work and developed by the Tavistock Institute, were valid and adequate. As institutions move into constricting circumstances, with tight boundaries, guarded exits, confused internal states and self-generated pollution by unsuspected negative feed-back effects, the resonance reaches down to similar patterns at the beginning of life. These are to be found, not in post-natal dynamics of human interaction, but in the impersonal

[1] L. de Mause, *The Journal of Psycho-history.* vol. iv, no. 3.

constricted confusions of intra-uterine existence. That fact constitutes the importance of this pre-natal model for institutional and group analysis.

Global Recession Must not Slip into Global Regression

The great danger is that, as many times before, we will interpret the fact of *recession*, on whatever scale or level it affects us personally, by evoking similar patterns of conflict and response from the past, that is by *regression*. If this happens, it will be a regression, not to post-natal, human levels of experience, but to pre-natal, first and third-trimester levels, of constrictions, threatening pressures, confused internal states and pollutions, and to similar patterns derived from even more crushingly frightening births. All these regressions belong to pre-personal levels, indeed to impersonal conflicts and resolutions.

If that happens within our family, social and institutional life, in Church and state, or globally (and some signs of its happening are already present), we could do one another great harm. We would confront each other, locked in impersonal blocks of force and counter-force, constricting and being constricted, polluting and being polluted, suffocating and being suffocated. Yet we would all feel quite justified in our fantasy-based cruelties, reacting to our fantasy dangers, because they would, following upon regression, be derived from impressions stored in pre-natal memory. The increasingly distressing, very real dangers, now being generated in present-day wombs, and the often forceps-assisted or rapidly induced births we provide for babies, will ensure a steady supply of damaged adults, who will see it all just as we do and carry on the carnage. Unless in the mercy of God we can learn to be more merciful, and in the humanity of Christ become more human, taking the pressure off pregnant mothers, this fate lies ahead for mankind.

Agitated and Anxious Depressions during the Birth

It was Stanislav Grof who first drew my attention to the dynamics of *retarded depression* as springing from the earliest stages of labour, when the cervix is still closed and there is immense pressure put on the organism, but with no room for manoeuvre and when no way out or exit has even suggested itself. The frequency of symptoms of compression and local bands of constriction in retarded depressive men confirm this observation.

He saw *agitated depressions* as having powerful dynamic roots in the next phase, when the cervix is opened, the womb elongated, and the foetal head travels forward, often in intense panic and discomfort, alternately struggling for life and sagging in total exhaustion. There tend to be frequent shortages of oxygen and in some cases real danger of suffocation, even if the cord does not happen to be stuck round the neck. The rage of the baby can rise to murderous heights as it struggles to survive against what feel like murderous pressures, with totally unreasonable demands, and as it tries to get out. It is infuriated at being pushed out at the same time as it is being held in, tighter than ever, with no instructions as to which way to turn. It is obvious that where a traumatic birth has been added to the constricted confusion of the first trimester, both will tend to reverberate into institutional pressures and transitions, leading to misperception, irrational, de-skilled responses and highly emotional violence, controlled or expressed. This knowledge is vital for counselling.

Implications for the Theology of Pastoral Care

Religions assert different qualities to be true of the gods they invite their followers to worship. In some, their gods are two-faced, like Janus, the god of January, the door of the year. He is both a 'closer and an opener'. We may like or dislike what he closes or what he opens. Some 'gods' or 'goddesses' are avowedly destructive and deadly, like Kali, the 'Black Mother'. Those who have been victims of severe intra-uterine distress would recognize her, with her four arms, blood-red palms and eyes, her matted hair and fang-like teeth, her necklace of skulls and girdle of snakes. Her worship at *Kali puja* requires bloody sacrifices.

The Christian faith is a proclamation that the God we respond to is the Creator of all things, and that as the Jewish-Christian story unfolds he is more and more discernible as a Father. He is to be thought of and responded to as to a Person who cares infinitely about justice and is especially concerned for whatever is easily hurt by careless strength, the very young and the old, the orphan and the widow, the poor and the sick. The 'Holy One of Israel', one of the names for God that describes his nature in the Book of Isaiah, has all these qualities. 'Holiness' is not distance, or transcendence meaning the inability of God to suffer, but closeness, immanence, the ability of God to be so closely identified with those of his covenant people who are victims of injustice as to warrant the statement 'in all their affliction he is afflicted'.

Metaphysical theologies have always had difficulty with this 'suffering servant' image of the 'holy one'. Their cosmology contrives to keep God out of the pain and the humiliating weakness with the result that, when they affirm that 'God', actually and inalienably, is already in the ground of every human being, it is as an unassailable focus of being, awareness and joy that he is there, quite removed from suffering.

The Christian faith, as the Church has understood its own experience of God, is of three Persons, the Father, the Son and the Holy Spirit. Christ, the Logos, the pre-existent Second Person of the Trinity, takes into himself the humanity of his creatures and 'becomes man' in Jesus Christ. Two natures are present in him, becoming or made wholly one in the task for which he was sent, of representing the love of the Trinity within human history and effecting a total deliverance through total reconciliation.

The Holy Spirit, the 'go-between God', attends, as it were, to the communications. Wherever the light and love, grace and empowering of the Holy Trinity are to operate, he as third Person is present alongside and within us. He it is who makes the Father and the Son real and actual in us, competent to effect the purposes of the Triune Godhead in a 'time' and history in which eternity has already been made present. The harshness of the affliction which an innocent foetus has often to endure, early in life in the womb, as outlined in this paradigm of human origins, calls for a much more exacting theological paradigm of reconciliation and reparation. Psychodynamic exploration has led us here. Can further exploration of the reconciling work of Christ match this depth, from the not-yet-searched-out riches of his justice?

The reconciling Word has come. In the Person of God the Father's fully human, reconciling Son, he speaks and acts into the clinical situation of cosmic suffering and pain. A clinical theology is constituted by his presence here with the sick. The Holy Spirit continues to apply the many-levelled work of Christ to individuals and groups, showing us the relevance of his Passion as our needs emerge.

Christ carried on his many functions, as Lord and Friend, Saviour and Companion, Priest and Counsellor, as Bread and Water of eternal life, as Shepherd and as Lamb, as King and Suffering Servant, under human conditions hedged about with multiple constrictions.

Because of the sharp divisions of verdict about him, he lived amid the confusions of love and hate, support and hostility. His experience of both constitutes his entitlement to be the Way, the Truth and the Life for us now.

The first experience of the cosmos may be so painful as to destroy the innate capacity to trust. Religions assert that God is, under certain conditions, trustable. The afflicted would like to trust him, but cannot. Jesus Christ asserts the steadfast love of the Father, and takes his own trust of him into hell. But paranoid-schizoid defences remain geared to suspicion or detachment. Those who suffer from them seldom get beyond 'trying to trust'.

God sets forth his Son to pioneer a 'ford' through this river of pain. Travel through it, from the position of painful withdrawal and distrust to open-hearted faith, becomes possible by his first making the journey. The turbulent waters remain, but the paralytic fear of the undertow, of being washed down and out to sea by the floods, is somehow removed.

The Task of Theodicy

In this way, the Father is 'justified'. The divine imperative to trust is seen to be both an essential element in the restoration of wholeness, and also just, in that God himself shows that the necessary way passes through the Cross. This is a function of what is called theodicy, how to speak well of God in the face of all the evil in his creation.

So, the deepening of the psychological paradigm to include the exigencies of the pre- and peri-natal journey, its dire circumstances, the daily impasse of having to depend on a source that is remembered as perpetually disappointing, requires a corresponding deepening of theodicy to cover it.

Where is this theodicy to be found? Among the 'not-yet-searched-out' riches of Christ in the scriptures. Among the commentators; here and there in inconspicuous corners in well-known theologians, from Ignatius and Irenaeus, through Augustine and Gregory Palamas to St John of the Cross, and on to Jurgen Molt-

mann and Pope John Paul II; in giants who straddle psychology
and theology as Søren Kierkegaard did, or pain-sensitized theologians such as F. D. Maurice, P. T. Forsyth, Simone Weil, Harry
Williams, Austin Farrer, Sebastian Moore, Rowan Williams, Henri
Nouwen, Kazoh Kitamori[2] and Kosuke Koyama.[3] Of these, both
the Japanese theologians base their theodicy on Martin Luther's
pivotal understanding of God's saving work as having first to cancel
out our misdirected efforts at salvation by frustrating them, revealing himself under contraries. God is best seen, for our essential
liberation and growth, when he is most 'hidden'.

The discovery that our basic, original injuries take place during
embryonic and foetal life, means that healing, if it is to be radical
and not just patched up, should take place at the same deep level.
Is that possible? Can healing be made retrospective, retroactive?
Can remedial work go back in time to reach and recompense the
primal sufferer for the wounding injustice of unmerited pain? If
reconciliation is to be effective in depth the recovery of the original
offence is necessary.

Repression Retains the Memory Intact

Paradoxically, this 'therapeutic regression' or deliberate going back
to put wrongs right is made easier, not harder, by reason of the fact
that the original wound is, or feels to be, as recent and raw now as
in the hour that it happened. Though in part split off from consciousness, dissociated and repressed, no detail of the incident has
been obliterated. The original 'taped' input was so threatening, in
view of the need to go on living in the same bad world, that it was
often further split into at least four 'tapes', each kept in separate,
'lead-lined cans'. Sensations, emotions, images, and concepts that
later find verbal utterance, are all 'gated-off' from one another.

By the same metaphor, it is now possible to play them back on
a 'mixer' with four inputs. The adult who is bent on achieving this
integration can bring the hurt child of the past into the present and
give it a voice.

---

[2] Kazoh Kitamori, *Theology of the Pain of God*. SCM Press, 1966.
[3] Kosuke Koyama, *Waterbuffalo Theology*. SCM Press, 1974.

Obstacles to Recall: Religion

Religion, in the broadest sense of 'piety' and 'loyalty' to parents, tends to obstruct a realistic recall. When Christian religion is associated, not, as in New Testament times, with the oppressed and under-privileged, but, as in the intervening centuries, is identified largely with ruling or privileged classes, an assumption creeps in that the prevailing order is a good one in which everyone feels, and ought to feel, 'good'. People who persistently 'feel bad' question, by their very existence, the many-levelled assumptions of the authorities that they are managing things in the best possible way for all concerned. The discontent of the actually oppressed is an offence to them. We see this constantly in the way 'respectable' families struggle to disown those of their family circle who become 'mentally ill'.

The Christian faith, denying its Founder and origins, has culturally assimilated this folk religion into its teaching and assumptions, subverting itself. Insofar as this has happened, it has involved a betrayal of the poor and the weak, the sick and the imprisoned, blatantly invalidating Christ's attitude of identification with the socially broken and disowned, subtly collaborating with his critics and murderers.

Promptings to Recall and Re-own the Weak and Failed Self

Christ existed as a sign not only in his 'earthly life', but also in his pre-incarnational life, as 'the Suffering Servant' and as 'the Holy One of Israel'. In both these implicit announcements of his coming, yet already present, Person, he draws attention to God's constant critique of the self-interest of those who happen to have the power and want to add to the luxury of its being good for them, the absurdity that it is good for everyone else.

The Transforming Presence

It seems to us to be quite necessary to use this christological resource for pre-natal or primal therapy (and for basic pastoral counselling for the healing of memories and for spiritual direction when they are working at equivalent depth). At times the 'facilitation' brought about by Christ's predictable presence with the afflicted is a conscious resource only in the hinterland of the counsellor's own personality. The name of God, the Son and the Spirit are, perhaps, not mentioned in the interview.

The Facilitation of an Adequate Theodicy

Nevertheless, these resources of our faith do get through to group-members. Christ becomes real precisely at the focal point of all the thorny questions of theodicy: 'How could a good God let such evil as this happen in a world for which he takes responsibility?'

These probing questions are answered by the presence of Christ alongside in equivalent catastrophic pain. He does not by any means deny or invalidate it or its offensiveness and scandal. Quite the contrary. He holds no brief for things as they are. He takes the whole constricted confusion on himself and uses it. He uses pain of all intensities as a prime medium in which he himself grew and enables us to grow.

The Human Dilemma Prompts God to Show the Way

The writer to the Hebrews makes this claim in the clearest possible way. 'It was appropriate that God, for whom everything exists and through whom everything exists, should make perfect, through suffering, the leader who would take them to their salvation' (Heb. 2:10 Jerusalem Bible). 'Since all share the same flesh and blood, he too shared equally in it, so that going through death as a man, he could destroy the power of the devil, who had death at his command, and set free all those who, through fear of death, had been in bondage all their lives' (Heb. 2:14–15). 'It was essential that he should in this way become completely like his brothers so that he could be compassionate and trustworthy in mediating the things of God to men and of men to God — the high priestly function' (Heb. 2:17). 'By God's grace he had to experience pain and death for every man' (Heb. 2:9).

Symbol, Metaphor and Image

The foetus deals with the invasion of maternal distress, the 'negative umbilical affect' as Mott called it, by a *symbolic* resistance to the badness of it. What we discover, in pre-natal integration work, is how this particular person, in his or her embryonic and foetal life, dealt with the invasion of badness. We watch where the line of battle against the black flood surged, what the 'last ditches' were, and whether any safe citadel could be found where the good foetal self could take refuge, to tend its wounds and from which to sally out again in hope, forgiving and, in spite of injuries, trusting again, relating again. *Different parts of the body are used symbolically to express this warfare.* Images and metaphors come to have decisive power in determining the outcome, and it is as such that the intra-uterine struggle and its defeats or prolonged running-battles enter the emotional and perceptual life of adults as profoundly distorting factors.

So when we look to theology, to some word from God to alleviate the complex situation, and if possible to do more, to reconcile thoroughly the whole adult-foetal person to the evil that intruded so soon after conception, that Word of God, to have any Logos power, any effective meaning, relevance and effectiveness, *will have to come in on the same level, as a reconciling symbol.* As metaphors that carry across reality from the Creator, making reparation to the innocent afflicted creature so as to re-establish trust, the images must be really representative of the personal identification of the Redeemer with those whose redemption is sought.

This, it has seemed to us for many years, is exactly what the Gospel of our Lord and Saviour Jesus Christ does. We saw it clearly when our focus, psychodynamically, was upon traumatic births and the dereliction of babies. Now that our sense of the bad experiences that have to be reached before they can be reconciled has gone deep into the first trimester of life in the womb, we find, as one would expect, that the Cross and Passion of Christ provide the reality of reconciling potential, in metaphors and symbolic images. These a clinical theology must explore and make available.

A Theology of Correlation

Our work is carried out for the most part among Christians alerted to their depth dimension by the Renewal, and humanists who have been similarly alerted by the Growth Movement. We have been led to recognize here close and significant correspondences between the two most common peri-natal catastrophes, the asphyxiating crushing afflictions of the birth process, and the separation anxiety which pushes the new-born to the limits of solitary pain and beyond, over the edge of the abyss into dereliction and a falling apart of the self in dread and non-being, and the two most terrible terminal experiences in the passion of Christ. He went through the crushing affliction of Gethsemane, the constricting agony, the bloody sweat and the struggle in the human will to go on into the horror or to draw back. He was victim to the flogging, the mockery and humiliation as all human rights were infringed. The crown of thorns (so like the crushing of the baby's head in to the hard bony circle of the pelvis, as several patients have remarked while undergoing it), was forced over his head. Finally, he staggered along the exhausting path to Calvary under the crushing weight of the wood across his neck and shoulders.

Then, so closely paralleling the primal dereliction of human infants as to be a marvel of appropriateness, he bore the loss of all friends, the pinioned anguish which could not in any way find relief for the mounting pain. The sense of social alienation and shame, the 'concatenation of confusion' as to who in this hell he was, came upon him. Was he the totally condemned man or the perfectly righteous one? Finally, he bore the dereliction which ended with the great cry from the Cross, 'My God, my God, why hast thou forsaken me?' (Matt. 27:46). The extension of the correlation, to match what we now know about the 'nail of affliction' where the mother's distress pierces the foetus and is displaced to the hands and feet, with the five wounds of Christ, the four nails and the spear, only increases our astonishment at the fittingness of it all.

The dereliction of infants after birth is worse and more unnatural than the crushing of birth. No blame can be attached to the parents for most abnormal deliveries. But when the newborn is denied an early opportunity to experience a mother's tender nearness, this failure of anyone to answer the urgent appeal for a presence gives rise to a deep inner horror. The terror is of a *deus absconditus*, a 'god' who has gone away, or is dead, perhaps killed. The reproach re-echoes in the mind, and in adult life still reverberates as a pervasive heartbreak. The basic question of theodicy, 'Is God to blame?' is avoided only by the infant's attributing the badness of the unbearable situation to some inexplicable but indelible badness in its own being. This is the usual outcome. It is unthinkable that 'the gods' are bad. Far better to take the blame and leave their righteousness intact. Parents are too powerful to dispute their handling of the situation.

But as Christians we have a God who 'is so near to us' (Deut.

4:7 R.S.V.) that he is both *deus crucifixus* and the God who absconds from himself, the *deus absconditus*, in the hidden mystery of Golgotha. This, says Luther, is the *deus theologicus*, and our knowledge of him crucified is shot through with paradox and contradiction.

An Inductive Theology

My task is to approach the work of Christ from the limited aspect of an inductive, strictly 'clinical' theology. I am not, as I understand my task, required to give a full and rounded account of the whole body of soteriological doctrine as such. I am not a teacher of theology. Approaching the theological task inductively, my concern must be to take up 'an issue in the present situation' and then to analyse it in depth, to see what is at stake in it and how Christian truth may be related to it. In keeping close to individual or family situations of need, in a joint search for God's specific remedy in Christ for these persons, we are being 'more scriptural and not less'.[4]

While my colleagues and I, as clinical theologians, have the duty of understanding thoroughly what we do and advising where advice is appropriate, we do not declare the whole saving counsel of God on each occasion. The whole pharmacopoeia of the Gospel as medicine is open to us to use. Our task is to move with the other person to the place where it becomes clear to one of us, or it is shown by the Spirit, what particular word, or insight, or meaning, clinches the matter in hand and makes the task clear. What we do stands or falls by its faithfulness to the juncture between the particular human need and a particular God-given resource, at whatever level.

We should expect to know more about the relevance of the Cross of Christ as we get to know more about man, since depth calls to depth. A new depth theology correlates with a new depth psychology. The Holy Spirit's work is to draw out truths about Christ which we have not recognized. The apostle who peered into the mystery and spoke of what he saw of 'the unsearchable riches of Christ' (Eph. 3:8 A.V.) would be astonished to learn that nearly 2000 years after his day, Christians are afraid of discovering treasures of wisdom simply because there is no clear precedent for them in his own writings.

[4] B. Kaye, (ed.), *Obeying Christ in a Changing World III*. Fontana. 1977.

What is Salvation?

But how is the liberation achieved through the reliving of the trauma of pregnancy and birth related to salvation in Christ? It depends what we mean by salvation. In many people the foetal distress and the trauma of birth are repressed and do not emerge into consciousness again until late adolescence, early adult life or even middle life. They emerge as a component in some dark night of the senses or of the spirit. They may emerge at a time of illness as a factor in breakdown. They may emerge at a time of abundant health, or indeed of the reception of baptism in the Holy Spirit, as the result of abundant grace that sweeps the cellars of the deep self clean. In this sense, a person may respond to the offer of the grace of Christ and enter salvation as a forgiven sinner while unconscious of this deeper dimension of innocent suffering.

In those who have always been afflicted from their youth onwards, this element of the saving work of Christ as theodicy will probably need to come in earlier. But whether earlier or later, I would consider it to be part of the saving work of Christ, and therefore an aspect of salvation. We do not have difficulty in experiencing both justification and sanctification as parts of salvation. It is perhaps in the area of sanctification that this work of Christ for innocent sufferers comes most into play. Sanctification means that the work of grace goes deep into the character structure, transforming and changing it. This is primarily to be received by faith as the life of Christ imparted to the human spirit. However, it is a common experience that this time of sanctifying is one of a profound shaking of the foundations. The human personality has its own rigid defences which do not readily give way.

The Healing of the Memories

The work of Michael Scanlan, reported in his book *Inner Healing*,[5] indicates that when a person comes time and again with the same besetting sin, his practice is not simply to hear the confession. He now calls upon the Holy Spirit to point up the area in the depth of the memory that is the source of this besetting sin. There then takes place a healing of the memories. Sometimes this is painless, sometimes it is exceedingly painful. In the former case the ego is not

[5] M. Scanlan, *Inner Healing*. New York, Paulist Press, 1974.

strong enough to bear the pain and Christ bears it all. In the latter, where the ego is strong enough and the context is favourable, the Spirit seems quite clearly to lead people into an actual reliving of the pain, within the power of the Saviour who shares it. It is my experience, and the experience of many others who have worked both in the Victorious Ministry movement and in clinical theology, that the cases in which pain is fully brought into consciousness and contextualized demonstrate the deeper, final and more finished work. But both give glory to God in Christ, the one simply, as in the Galilean ministry, the other paradoxically, as in the ministry of Christ from Tabor to Golgotha.

There is in some people an anxiety lest healing as described here should be equated with the work of salvation. As pastoral counsellors, dealing with those who are emotionally sick, our work is somewhat like that of the mission hospital. Our work is to practise the works of love rather than to preach the Word of life. In fact we do both, and I find myself speaking the Word of life much more frequently than I did as a medical missionary commissioned to do the works of love.

There has been some suspicion that we have equated the reliving of birth as part of this healing of the memories with the experience of the new birth into the family of God by faith in Christ. It is of course not the case and would be ridiculous if it were so. There is, however, a close relationship between their physical birth and the ways in which people experience difficulty or ease when they come to consider whether they can accept the new birth by faith into Christ. All the fears, doubts and commitment anxieties that beset them at their physical birth tend to crowd round people at the proposal of a second birth. Indeed, to force oneself towards the experience of being born again into the family of God can evoke primal disturbances of psychotic intensity, if the actual gestation and birth were accompanied by pain of mind-splitting character. Just as Christ healed people physically but left them to decide later what they would do by way of faith and discipleship, so, if we can clear a way through the living debris of the first womb and the first birth, we do at least make it possible for a person to consider the second birth and the womb of the Spirit without the degree of panic and confusion, resistance and dread which accompanied the first.

CHAPTER 4

The Pastoral Counsellor and Religious Faith

The Use and Misuse of Religion

Counselling is correctly assumed to be an activity open to anybody to undertake. Correctly, because when a person is asked for advice or persuaded to listen, whatever that person says by way of reply is counselling. To remain silent would be equivocal: it could be the best counsel, or the worst, or halting between two opinions.

To counsel professionally is a different matter. The question then arises, 'By what right do I offer counsel? Who vouches for me?' I am a member of the Royal College of Psychiatrists; but would what I practise meet with their approval? In a tight corner, from where do I derive my resources? On certain matters I might well consult a colleague who is a member of the College. In other matters I would have more confidence in my spiritual director, or in prayer.

Some might ask what the relationship is between membership of the Royal College of Psychiatrists and the tested capacity of that member as a counsellor or therapist. Knowing the quite negative attitudes to psychotherapy and counselling that have sometimes been promulgated by members of that prestigious institution of psychiatrists, an inquirer might press me with the challenge that the same psychiatric qualification could be held by a person rather hostile to counselling, doubting the value of so-called 'therapeutic dialogue'. In some cases my roots in psychiatry give confidence to clients, but on other occasions I have to prove myself a person who can be trusted in spite of the stable that trained me.

Some people who need help are more concerned about my beliefs than about my professional qualifications. People's hold on their faith in God may well be weakened at a time of depression. It can be totally obscured. Yet there may be enough of the competent 'Adult' still functioning in them to make them quite certain that they do not wish to abandon their tenuous faith as a condition of return to health. When a young doctor, for instance, gives up a pressured adherence to the religion his parents forced on him, it is probably a neurotic attitude which he is giving up, not true belief. Genuine belief is seldom surrendered, whatever blows life deals out. The 'beliefs' of a young doctor or psychiatrist, time-bound and culturally conditioned, might be in external religious practices which it is an act of integrity to reject. But it may be the genuine core of ultimate meaning to the whole of life for one of his patients.

I never find myself threatened by hostility to religion in those who consult me: quite the reverse. The 'God' they are refusing to believe in is one I would not like to have to believe in myself. It is not 'pure religion and undefiled' (Jas. 1:27 A.V.) that they have given up. It is often necessary to desert a naïve and unparadoxical religion before it is possible to face up to the realities of the task of maturing, or the task of integrating the complexities of life in middle age and advancing years. So I desire in some way to declare my conviction about God's revelation of our true humanity through Christ. My philosophy of counselling, which derives from that belief, approves, nevertheless, the primacy of listening. Hurt people have a greater need to meet a God who hears and groans, who struggles for words, than a God who has much to say to them.

There is too extensive an overlap in psychiatric practice between psychodynamics and what is broadly known as religion, for me to agree with those who would claim that a man's religious stance is of no consequence in his practice of psychotherapy and counselling. Even our silences selectively affirm or implicitly question the roots and courses of actions and feelings which we discuss with our clients in the course of counselling.

By working under the auspices of the Clinical Theology Association, and making it clear that it is a Christian theology that we mean by this title, it is clearly established that those who consult us will find us friendly to a genuine faith. The way they are using their faith may be shot through with misunderstandings that are so serious in the present circumstances that their unbalanced beliefs and unreal expectations play a large part in making them sick and keeping them so. For instance, a person who is deep in the experi-

ence of depressive unworthiness and guilt usually makes quite er-
roneous statements about God and his attitude to them. Or when
obsessional reactions predominate, some people are compelled to
strive to do 'what God wants them to do' and carry it out so
scrupulously that I recognize in them a sick faith. Even so, my aim
is to build up a sound faith which will correct these distortions.

I remember, for example, a neat belligerent woman, who spoke
and moved as though she might have left her horse in the drive,
warning me at our first meeting that if I dared talk about God she
would walk out. I agreed pleasantly that she was free to express
her disapproval in that way, just as I or anyone else was free to
talk about, or not talk about, anything under the sun or beyond it.
On the second day of one of our conferences she was reliving the
oppression of her spirit as a child by a particularly insensitive and
seemingly obnoxious father. The character reference she gave him
was in no way complimentary. It struck me that her father was
showing all the defects she had attributed to God; but I said nothing
of this. Suddenly, with a cross between a chuckle and a guffaw, she
broke out, 'It's this father of mine I have been complaining about.
I have got to be fair. Let's get God off the hook, shall we?'

On the third and final afternoon we were facing the 're-entry'.
Having lived in a real, mostly honest, and caring community for
three days, the unreal world, often unkind and generally too busy
to listen, was at the home end of a few hours' journey. As I had not
noticed her mounting impatience it was quite an unexpected moment for me when she suddenly blurted out in front of the group,
'For goodness sake, why don't we pray? We're going to need God
to face this lot. Get praying, will you!' This spirited woman had
meant to put me in a tight corner by her initial injunction to keep
God out of my speech. My respect for her freedom had not included
intimidation on either side. This dénouement was a delight. The
whole group, with her at the centre of it, broke into laughter,
enjoying the joke played upon her former self by the good gift of
true insight.

It is important to many of those who consult me that I base my
own life and thought on what they believe are Christian realities.
It is important to me, in my turn, not to be expected to drag God
into every second sentence in order to reassure someone weak in
the faith that God has not been forgotten. I prefer not to have a
matter-of-fact interview interrupted by religious clichés and catch

phrases. Words that are true are good and godly in an intrinsic fashion that needs no embroidering. It does not seem to me that God requires us to advertise his presence by frequently referring to him. As spiritual teachers have constantly said, God obscures his presence. Living with his silence is as important to maturity as obeying his word. I therefore resist the demand of those who want me to console them with some form of fashionable words held in high esteem in their particular wing of the church. Such words have become shibboleths and doctrinal passports to what is only, after all, a cultic acceptance.

In marital problems one discovers not infrequently the partner who interlaces the conversation with continual allusions to biblical texts and scriptural phrases to be the one who is refusing to look at the simple realities of his human relationship; while the partner who has become allergic to the God-talk is in fact the one who understands the real difficulties that lie between them. Handling this is a tactical matter. I want to stem the flood of pious platitudes so that the God of truth may be heard speaking, as the partners learn to speak in simple human terms about what is going on between them. This strategy of enabling them to hear together the truth, which is God's truth about their relationship, demands a tactic that seems to run in opposition to the common ministerial strategy.

The Relationship Between the Science of Psychology and Faith

The autonomy of science is no threat to faith or religion so long as the fields in which they are working are sufficiently removed from one another. But when the area of investigation includes the ultimate ends and moral means of human life itself, territory which has traditionally belonged to religion, and within which Christian theology has already achieved a large measure of integration, the risk of dispute and eventual disagreement is inevitable. Following Kierkegaard, the Christian objection is not to the scientific method applied to matters in which it can be competent and can increase its competence. The quarrel is entirely in defining the frontiers of the territory within which the unaided scientific method can reasonably expect to be competent. The ultimate question is: can we know everything by ourselves, or are there matters which, in the very nature of things, are going to require revelation?

The Hegelian vision of man left no room for faith in revelation. There was no need for it. No limit could be assigned to the capacity of human reason to establish all that could or should be known by man about himself. Reason, operating upon observation and with logic, could discover the nature and the destiny of man. Intelligence could find God, if any God there were to be discovered. Science could discover what people needed in order to be made happy. Provided they were reasonable and listened to the new experts on being human, science could organize their contentment.

In contemporary neuro-physiological terms it is as if the 'enlightened' left-hemispherical rationality, arrogant rather than humble in its scientifically élitist yet fashionable humanism, cannot submit to the possibility of a superior vision, or to wisdom being granted to some unlettered individual on the basis of an intuitive right-hemispherical vision. The vaunted schemes of liberation designed by the expert scientific liberators cannot conceive of a freedom that comes from another direction altogether. Even if there is some substance in Christ's claim to bring freedom to men when they take up his Cross and share his risen life, the wisdoms of this world can never regard that claim as other than foolish.

The task of a Christian philosophy of science and knowledge in any generation is to press human reason to its proper limits and then to use the wisdom which God gives us by the Holy Spirit, expounding Christ to us, to bring insight and understanding to all those matters which the order of science cannot reach. In our generation I know of no writer with a broader grasp of these problems than Bernard Lonergan in his study of human understanding, entitled *Insight*.[1] His concern is 'to reach the act of organizing intelligence that brings within a single perspective the insights of mathematicians, scientists, and men of common sense'. He is attempting an insight into insight. He sees insight as an apprehension of relations and meanings. He believes that it yields a synthetic account of all our thinking. Insight unifies and organizes and yields a philosophy and a metaphysics.

Lonergan recognizes that we must undertake the task of understanding with total seriousness, and attempt to express what we are persuaded is true, in order that others may, hopefully, be brought to an acceptance of the same truth by our persuasiveness. But there

[1] B. Lonergan, *Insight*. Darton, Longman and Todd 1957.

remains the fact of evil, which finally overturns the Greek optimism, which assumed that people had only to understand in order to act, and that when their ignorance was brought into the light by knowledge, they would act according to the light.

This is a thoroughly dialectical situation, in which we are saying enthusiastically both 'yes' and 'no' to the task of thoughtful investigation of all that lies before us in counselling, using our best intelligence to illuminate the issues, while at the same time admitting that the very instruments we use, our own intelligence and mental faculty, are as badly damaged as the rest of us.

The scientist naturally finds it harder to distrust intelligent reasoning, which is the main instrument for making progress, than does the man whose faith in God's revelation makes him more open to the fact that his rationality is mixed with much unconscious irrationality and flight from understanding.

There are strong reverberations of this basic difficulty in the division between the two wings of mental health in Britain, particularly in psychiatry itself. Our orthodox psychiatry is closely allied in its philosophy to general medicine with its immense record of progress, based on the need for scientific inquiry to press ahead with its own investigations and under its own authority, to the very limits of its territory and beyond. This approach of 'organic' psychiatry has good reason to be proud of the results of intellectual research.

Psychiatrists on the other wing of our discipline tend to be called 'dynamic' because of their concern with intra-psychic and interpersonal transformations, which have more to do with the emotions than with the reason. They are traditionally more aware of the limitations of reason. It is not only in their patients that they observe irrationality but also in themselves, and even in their organically-minded colleagues.

The pastoral counselling task intends to help people break free from their chains. In order to do this, we should know as much as possible about the nature of these chains, their strengths, their points of attachment, their weak links, and know all this as systematically and scientifically as possible. This knowledge, whether shared with the other person or not, is a useful adjunct and precursor to this bid for freedom.

Our authority as counsellors ought to consist partly in the accuracy with which we have related ourselves to the scientific understanding of man and woman which has taken place and which is still taking place. The pastoral counsellor aims to be in good enough contact with psychology, which deals in man's temporal dynamics. But we also bear in mind the eternal and unchanging authority of the Word of God. We must, unless we live in a fantasy world, relate ourselves to contemporary claims that the human sciences have changed our interpretation of that unchanging Word so drastically that even many theologians now despair of deriving firm ethical norms from the scriptures. Our position as authorities, even for the conduct of our own lives, has become dialectical. 'Yes, but . . .' is often on our lips when challenged to take our stand by a client who insists on our being concrete and definitive.

Christians who come for counselling can feel threatened when the counsellor speaks from the authority of that body of knowledge he has had handed down to him, the 'findings' of psychology and psychiatry, or of some other scientific discipline. Counsellees who are themselves highly qualified scientists, and who require me to respect the authority of the body of knowledge represented by their particular discipline, are, both rightly and wrongly, apt to quibble and become extremely 'biblical', even quoting texts at me, if the interpretation based on psychology is not to their liking. They are, in fact, behaving like those medieval church authorities who resented and resisted every attempt of scientists to become independent of theologians. They want the Bible and revelation to say all that can be said on the matter before us.

All of us who are Christians in caring professions are committed to what emerges from well-conducted research in our field. Those results must be respected. The law of contingency implies that if you search for facts and their relationship and come up with findings, you will give weight to those results. When secular sciences and Christian experience cover roughly the same area, discrepancies will arise and may well be real. But so far, in my own professional experience, the discrepancies have proved to be apparent rather than real.

The Pastoral Counsellor and Mystical Experience

I have a deep desire to validate where possible the religious experience of my many contemplative friends, Western and Eastern, for whom Christ is only one Word of God among many. I am consulted by young and middle-aged people who are well into the practice of contemplative mysticism of one kind or another. My counselling work involves me in helping them make discriminations in this field.

In our primal work in residential conferences it is not uncommon for men and women to achieve a creative regression to the 'ground of being', as first experienced by them in the week between their conception and the implanting of the zygote in the wall of the uterus. How they do this we have very little idea. That they do it becomes increasingly evident. They speak of going back to an astonishing sense of being perfectly self-subsistent, of radiant wholeness and blessedness, of 'being', of 'awareness' and 'joy', of having God and the universe within this perfect sphere which they feel themselves to be.

Indeed, this was precisely their blastocystic condition. Those who have been drawn to a certain kind of contemplative activity spontaneously identify the unitive experience there with the experience of their primal work with us. It is they who make this interpretation, not I. But it makes very good sense of so much of the language of mysticism about regaining contact with a long-lost source of unity with God who is at the ground of our being. Here there is no division between masculinity and femininity; there is no obvious dichotomy between good and evil; the fall has not yet occurred and there is nothing to strive for. There are no parental images. No ego-states or defences have as yet been developed. Suddenly they seem to have a new and substantial grasp of a mystical state which has always drawn them, but has usually escaped their grasp except for moments of peak experience. This actual experience, with its sensations and emotions and its original context apparently clearly identified, sheds for them new light on what has always seemed an appropriate religious quest.

It may be disconcerting, but the phenomenological parallels between this blissful week between conception and implantation, and the statements of the mystics of the great ethnic religions raise some important questions. Having claimed to be a Christian counsellor I am inevitably pressed into careful discernment. It may be, as some Catholic mystical writers would suggest (and in doing so find support from the mystics of other traditions for the pursuit of ego-loss and union with the Absolute) that this is essential Christianity. God may choose, and maybe always has chosen, to reveal himself to every world religion through these esoteric aspects, so that those who achieve the contemplative vision are, so to speak, the spiritual aristocracy, leading man to higher states of spiritual evolution. In India it would certainly be correct to make such a statement on behalf of the rishis who have disciplined themselves to retain a sense of union with the Absolute. However, the Christ whom these esoteric mystical writers so eagerly reduce in order to assimilate him to their list of Logos-figures, avatars and saviours, is no longer the unique Christ of the Letters to the Hebrews or the Ephesians.

The founder of transpersonal psychology, Abraham Maslow, emphasized the importance of peak experiences of a mystical kind and felt they represented the higher reaches of spirituality open to the human race. Nevertheless, he warned his readers that there were dangers in pursuing this mystical experience. The main danger he recognized was 'of making action impossible or at least indecisive.'[2] This form of cognition is without judgement, comparison, condemnation or evaluation. Also it is without decision, because decision is readiness to act, and . . . this is passive contemplation, appreciation, and non-interfering, i.e. "let be".'[3] These states, for a while, may make a person unable to act. They tend to make a person less responsible, especially towards helping other people. They tend to fatalism; what will be, will be. 'The world is as it is; it is determined; I can do nothing about it.' They can lead, says Maslow, 'to undiscriminating acceptance, to blurring of everyday values, to too great tolerance'.[4]

In these states of primal perfection, a person may not only perceive himself as perfect, at least in some sense, but also see other people in ways which can be fallacious. If he makes the retention of this experience his goal, he is probably not fitting himself for responsible living. Since contingency is an imperfection, the mystic tends to regard the whole world of historical striving as *maia*, or illusion.

In Buddhism and in many esoteric religious groups there has been an awareness of this world-devaluing tendency, and a reaction against it towards some kind of positive valuation of human life and recognition of the need for loving service of others. Yet, even for them, evil can be regarded as but an aspect of the good. The reality

---

[2] A. Maslow, *Toward a Psychology of Being*. Van Nostrand.
[3] Ibid.
[4] Ibid.

of sin can evaporate for those who take their cue from these blissful experiences. The identity they derive from them tends towards the divinization of the self. But this is not the biblical sense, where sinners, rescued by the Cross of Christ, are drawn into sonship in the family of God, being made 'sons and heirs of God' (Gal 4:7). World mysticism does not speak so. This state of blessedness is not reached for such people by forgiveness, justification and sanctification, or by faith in God's declared intention to establish a community of sharing in the divine life. Though they would claim that it is a gift of God, the mystic path is one which is taught by the teacher to those who accept his methods and techniques of prayer, in order to attain to this divinity. This is reached by breaking through to something which, by their account, is essentially present in every person.

The Re-evaluation of Primal Bliss

My own sense of the matter is that there is great therapeutic gain when people are able to discover that so blissful an experience of being, awareness and joy is, as the mystics have always claimed, actually part of their own experience. This becomes a positive asset, especially if they were, in the subsequent months of life in the womb, at birth or afterwards, subject to severe deprivations and injuries. To rediscover this sense of primal unitive blessedness is precious. When it is reached as a result of primal therapeutic regression, however highly it is valued, it is unlikely that Christian people will be tempted to spend the rest of their lives attempting to stay in this state of mind, however superior it is to the turmoil of daily living. They are unlikely to turn what is excellent archaeology into what, from the Christian point of view, could be a disastrous teleology. Those who work with us and wish to remain firmly within the context of Christian prayer will not extrapolate a theology of supernatural grace from this unexpectedly blissful experience. The conditions under which they have access to it, and their clear sense of its actual original context, tend to lead them to the place where they regard it as blessedly natural rather than supernatural. It is certainly part of the cosmic work of Christ as God's agent in creation that, at the very beginning of existence, there should be this utterly glorious sense of pristine unitive being.

Glad of such blissful beginnings, the Christian will proceed to take up the tasks to which Christ calls him in discipleship, making his response to the call of Christ as his contemporary, to a discipline which gives weight to the eternal seriousness of our actions in history. Such a focus is foreign to the esoteric philosophies. In many cases those who have achieved the retrieval of this primal blessedness proceed to experience terrible deprivations during the later months of intra-uterine life. They may have to endure long and lonely wilderness states in the womb of the mother who totally rejects their presence. She imparts to them her own miseries. They may need all the power of the Holy Spirit who stayed with Christ during his own wilderness temptations, and when he came to his own and his own did not receive him (John 1:11), if they are to assimilate and carry through that original unitive glory into life beyond birth.

Others require the assistance of Christ and the Holy Spirit to enable them to overcome the trauma of birth. There would seem to be some evidence that excessively severe birth trauma can so totally destroy the will of the baby to endure this process of agonizing birth, that there is a turning back, a desire to return to the beginning. It happens even before birth has been completed. It may be that one of the great enabling functions of the Cross of Christ is to make it possible for those who are in revulsion at the horror of life, dependent upon the flesh, on woman, on the contingencies of human life and its miserable history, to forgo their absorption with the blessedness with which they began.

I am ready to discuss with those who consult me and do primal work in our groups these philosophical, religious and theological issues. This by no means determines the outcome for the individual person. Some with whom I have talked on such things have remained dedicated to the path of 'natural mysticism'. For them it remains supernatural, and their probable journey to India has its own logic. Others have become aware of these discriminations and have decided to place the burden of their salvation not upon the attainment of these blessed states, but upon the redemptive work of Christ, giving him the primacy which is characteristic of the Letter to the Ephesians (Ephes. 1:10), and the 'better sacrifices, better priesthood and better saviourhood' of the Letter to the Hebrews.

The Place of the Eucharist in Healing

Since Christ has himself entered into our condition at its best and at its worst, in its joy and in its agony, the broken body and blood of Christ as understood in the Eucharist are a basic remedy which enables reconciliation at depth to be achieved. I would feel deprived and unsettled if at least one day of our residential conferences did not begin with the Holy Communion. I need to feed upon the realities which will enable me and others to go boldly throughout the day into the most mind-shattering corners of our human catastrophe.

On our conferences, there is no doubt about the objective reality of this sacramental meal and God's objective work through it. It roots the individual in the redemptive work of Christ, sharing suffering, and sharing the joy that comes through full endurance.

The concept has often been canvassed that those who gather for the worship of God, expressing their openness to resources beyond themselves, are 'representative'. What they gain by the 'inward' movement, meeting a resourceful God at the appointed place, they then carry out into their communities in such a way that the benefits are spread to the whole community, including those who have not worshipped. Non-attenders are represented by those who attend. I am being brought round to the soundness of that notion through what is expressed by those who do not worship with us. They speak of a powerful sense of an over-arching protection and strength, of firm gentleness and characteristically Christian grace, which pervades the day in ways they cannot account for.

Those who stay away from the liturgy do so for different reasons. It is not uncommon for clergymen to feel, for once, 'off duty'. The mildly rebellious who still have God twisted up in a knot, long ago tied too tightly by the relentless religion of their parents, are still in a state of reaction. It seems better that they express this by absence until Christ's invitation speaks to them: 'If any man thirst, let him come' (John 7:37 A.V.). For others it is the first time they have attended the Eucharist. In this context we do not use it as an exclusive service, 'for members only'. It is more relevant to remember the purpose Christ's own words give it, 'a showing of the Lord's death until he comes' (1 Cor. 11:26).

The passion and death of Christ, with the resurrection and the giving of the Holy Spirit are, in our experience, intimately and specifically related to the healing ministry of the Church, especially where what is to be healed is mental pain of great intensity. As we now understand it, the worst pain is inflicted in intra-uterine life and the early days of babyhood. There are tight corners here, for counselling and psychotherapy, which I would not have dared even to approach unless I had sensed that we were being led and sent as disciples into places which Christ well knew and had visited, and meant to visit again in the tortured spirits of his children. In this context I wish to share some of my thoughts which gather round the Holy Eucharist.

The Anglican eight o'clock communion of my youth, in our country parish of Aughton in Lancashire, was reverent and quiet, useful for the chorister like myself who could be too attentive to the music to be able to concentrate on the meaning of the later services. You could rely, at this early service, on not being disturbed by others' looks. We saw only each others' backs, and the back of the Rector for most of the time. There was no sermon and no attempt at church-door bonhomie. There were no concessions at all to subjectivity, emotions, personal interaction, dialogue or meeting. We went home as untouched and unattended to humanly as when we arrived.

A recent paper by a Jungian analyst referred to an investigation which showed that over eighty per cent of Jungian analysts belonged to what Jung himself would call the introverted type, as against only twenty-five per cent in the general population. I would guess that most of us who found that early communion congenial were introverted types. It may be that some of us were even burdened with personality hurts which led to our disliking the kind of fellowship and extravert activity from which that particular service protected us. For these reasons some of us found it hard to accept the parish communion when it became the central service of the day. The early service enabled us to keep in contact with some of the Christian realities without in any way disturbing our defences.

In my adolescence I was unaware of the possibilities of meeting my fellow worshippers either humanly or mystically. I could not have conceived in those days the quality of divine-human enrichment which I now know in the Series Three Eucharist in the company of friends and fellow-workers. Nowadays we are gathered in a circle, intently aware of each person's expression. We delight in common membership of the body of Christ, at times aware of helplessness and anguish in others, looking forward to the resolution of their pain. Here I sense that my feet are set in a large room. Here, above all, tight corners resulting from the various pressures we have to negotiate are not just tolerable, they are exhilarating.

When I write in this way, some will perhaps object to me as an innovator, introducing elements into eucharistic practice which have no place there. Yet the objective act and our participation in it are central for me. To give room for the Holy Spirit to break in with something new and unique, something he may want to give to a particular person or a particular group, is not in my view to deviate from the Last Supper which Jesus celebrated with his friends. In fact it may well be that this is more faithful to what was happening that first Thursday evening. We do not find that this style of Eucharist, in which there is a particular focus on what God is doing by way of transformation for one of his sons or daughters present, detracts at all from the central act of remembering the death of Christ.

I would like to share some thoughts on the discourses at the Last Supper. For Christ himself this was indeed a tight corner. Our participation in his way of handling it is the secret of our safe passage, when the tight corners of the foundation months of our lives have to be negotiated as part of a necessary healing.

The Last Supper with the 'Wonderful Counsellor'

The Last Supper of Christ and his disciples, like that of the early Christian Church, was not itself the Passover, or even the continuation of the Passover. There was no lamb on the table, nor the four cups. The ordinary word for bread is used – not that for unleavened bread which would be used on the next day, the Passover. The objective action, once for all, full, perfect and sufficient, took place on Calvary. The Last Supper points to that event, in the words of the institution spoken by our Lord, 'This is my body, broken . . . my blood, shed.' The subjective aspect, 'what it means to me, personally, and to you, my friends', was the main content of the conversation which Jesus initiated. St John records what they spoke about at that meal. Our celebration comes short of Christ's intention if our own style is impersonal and one-sidedly 'objective'.

At that last evening meal with his disciples, Christ was looking already to the great cosmic sacrifice which he would, on the next day, or day of the Crucifixion, complete and make available as the new ground of relatedness between God and man. He was also looking ahead to the effect of all these coming events on his friends. He talked over with them the disturbing, bewildering, emotional paradoxes into which they would be plunged as they followed him. Their joy would be mixed with sorrow. Judas would use his freedom to betray him; Peter, bragging, disinclined to have his feet washed, would deny him. Thomas, at that meal, spoke out of the distinctive difficulty of his logical but limited personality. 'If we don't know X, how can we know Y that follows from it?' Philip, always eager, reassured Jesus that if only they could be shown the Father as Jesus saw him, they would believe. And the other Judas, a normally silent man, asked his one recorded question at the Last Supper, 'Lord how is it that you will manifest yourself to us and not to the world?' Why is this revelation not open to the inspection of neutral observers? Men demand data over which they have some power of command. They want to decide on the basis of facts, cool facts which can be kept at a distance, free from emotional loading, with no prior commitment.

In all this, Christ exemplified sensitive and acute empathy. His perception of what they were feeling and thinking was accurate. He expressed it in words which they would at least remember, until hard experience brought understanding home to them. This is unmistakably effective 'crisis counselling'.

Chapter 16 of the Johannine discourses opens with the words, 'I have said all this to you to keep you from falling away' (R.S.V.). He envisaged their crises. It is an explanation from Jesus which shows his awareness of the likely effect of the way he had been directed to go about saving the world from the power of evil, triumphing over it by submitting to it at its worst. The counsellor's provision of 'immediacy', that is, 'what is going on between us now', is exemplified as Christ, envisaging the offensiveness of this way of the Cross, acknowledged that they would be tempted to fall away from following him. But with this possibility and warning, and by the Spirit's life in them, reminding them of all Jesus had said, they would be forearmed.

On the Thursday evening at the supper of friends, Christ prepared them to live in an upside-down world, where 'the greatest will be the servant of all' (Matt. 23:11). Any self-serving, self-seeking power, even in high places, would be judged. The mighty would be put down from their seat.

In counselling the question should not be asked: 'How quickly and completely can I understand this person's inner and hidden problem, so that with equal speed and completeness I can confront the other with the truth about himself?' The counsellor's problem is rather: 'How much of the truth that I discern can they bear just now? How can I make the painful truth bearable?' This is exactly what was in the mind of Christ. He had to temper the objective truth which his disciples could not bear subjectively. 'I have yet many things to say to you, but you cannot bear them now' (John 16:12 R.S.V.). The Holy Spirit would, however, declare the mind of God and of Christ to his disciples in the future, enabling them to bear the truth and to overcome their defensive, subjective fears.

They questioned one another: 'We do not know what he means.' Jesus knew what they wanted to ask him, so he said to them, 'Is this what you are asking yourselves, what I meant by saying . . .' (John 16: 18–19 R.S.V.) 'Truly, truly, I say to you, you will weep and lament, but the world will rejoice; you will be sorrowful, but your sorrow will turn into joy . . . and no one will take your joy from you.' (John 16:20, 22 R.S.V.). This is characteristic counselling discourse. He took up their confusion as to what he meant, and reassured them that sorrow, thoroughly endured in the service of truth, would change into an abiding joy.

My meditation on the conversations of Christ with his disciples before, during and after his communion meal with them, sustains my belief in the appropriateness of counselling discourse before, during and after our communion meals now. It is here pre-eminently that Christ manifested his charisma as a pastoral counsellor, with all the endowment of the Spirit giving to his words and his wisdom deep penetration and power. Christ did not use that power to prevent his followers from gaining insight into themselves by avoiding painful experiences of failure. Nor does he now. Nor should we attempt to improve on his performance by over-protectiveness, or naïvety, or triumphalistic avoidance of pain in ourselves and in those we counsel.

What we do 'in remembrance' of him, recalling his last meal with his disciples, departs from the original insofar as, by striving too hard for liturgical objectivity alone, we discourage those specific personal responses. By means of those particulars its relevance for all is manifested. The sharing of current experiences by some of the participating laity promotes the original purpose of the meal.

CHAPTER 5

Identification and Individuality

Identification with the Client

Carl Rogers, one of the most influential teachers of counselling, is said to have recommended to his students his own practice, just before a new patient entered his consulting room, of walking to the window and in some symbolic way, throwing out of it all his long-amassed stores of knowledge. Only then did he feel safe to turn round and face the new-comer with the necessary openness, receptiveness and attentiveness. He knew the subtle danger of the professional's anxiety about the level of his performance. It is not only beginners who let themselves become over-eager to match the patient's baffling questions with correct and competent answers. Anxiety of that sort is a distraction from the real task. It shifts the focus of attention from the client's concerns to those of the counsellor. The interview is then being used to treat the therapist's anxieties, protecting his or her self-esteem and guarding against his or her loss of face.

At times, this has been seen as a direct conflict between competence in the form of knowledge, and skill in maintaining a focused attention. To see this as a confrontation between alternatives is mistaken. One of the fruits of a well-rooted training is the kind of many-levelled awareness that allows our main focus to rest on the task of listening to, seeing and sensing the other person with all the antennae we possess. We focus our attention on the other person, while at the same time our peripheral attention ranges over many additional observations. These include some which come from within ourselves. Training provides us with automatic sorting boxes into which bundles of assorted facts habitually fall. The purpose of counsellor education is to familiarize us with syndromes, or 'what-commonly-goes-with-what' in recognizable patterns. Behind syndromes are more-or-less predictable common origins or causes. Here individual variation overlaps with the common lot of human beings. There is an infinite variety of ways of being healthy. But if there were not, broadly speaking, a limited number of ways of being ill, the task of doctors in bringing to bear their past experience of diagnosing and treating similar 'cases' would be made impossible.

Pastoral care need not be so wedded to the uniqueness of each person as to refuse to pay attention to similarities and syndromes. It is as we recognize these patterns that the experience of the ages can be harnessed for the use of the person who has come with today's burden of confusion and bewilderment. He hopes we can make sense of at least some part of it. And so we can, if we allow this process of concurrent alerting of association areas in the brain to go on. This scanning process initiates and facilitates a search along all possibly relevant tracks, gently inhibiting those which seem to be irrelevant, instinctively weighing up the likely emotional loading of such positive findings as come to light. Having made a link with some recognizable pattern of events we then have to decide how best to share this, so as not to prejudice its acceptance, nor to over-persuade, but simply how to gain a fair hearing.

At times, this concurrent reflection of ours reaches a block. Our insearch leads to no light on the matter. No elucidating patterns emerge. We no more understand what is going on than our client does, possibly much less.

What we do then determines the whole future course of our joint enterprise. The baffled person hands on to us the bewilderment experienced from life, which is itself often based on the primary confusions he or she felt as a small child seeking, without success, meaning and basic answers from parents. We are made to feel the same mixture of frustration, guilt, loss of self-esteem, cluelessness and even stupidity that he has felt all along, and increasingly of late. The crucial issue is upon us. Does our repertory of responses to such feelings of helplessness include any reserves of courage and resource, not by denying the impasse, but by a power of inclusion? Does our level of self-acceptance enable us to remain undefended in the presence of the same total bewilderment, notwithstanding the other person's expectation of us as repositories of comprehension?

Are we able to stay with the mystery, and avow its present impenetrable character? If we can, though our shared bafflement remains unaltered, its disintegrating, belittling effect on the baffled person will have been transformed, and its ill-effects probably abolished.

Whether we have that resource or not, certainly we are in a tight corner here. Our main focus of attention can still be on the other person. But our concurrent reflection must be able to continue noiselessly dealing with our own dilemma. We are now in the presence of our own personal problem. How do we deal with a threatened loss of face and diminished self-esteem? How do we re-route this potentially disastrous internal message, that we too have reached the end of our resources, that our own search has failed, that our own attempt to find a way out is as blocked as that of the person before us, whose similar blockage led to a breakdown? If we cannot re-circulate the message of personal defeat, impeded progress, and blocked forward momentum, there is a real risk of its hooking on to our own experiences of the same pattern (as, for example, from an obstructed drive to get born) with a resultant deep depression in ourselves.

Trifocal Lenses

We are always in search of analogies when what we are struggling to convey is out of the ordinary. The notion of bifocal or trifocal spectacles is attractive. I am sitting three or four feet away from the other person. I focus upon him with my middle-distance lens. But as he speaks, I sometimes become aware of the long distance lens picking up some known or presumed patterns in his dim past which are almost identical to those he is telling me about. As they flow over him in the here and now, he is at a loss to understand them even though he senses a repetitious quality about them. He feels that he is being lived by forces over which he has no control. His adult decisions miscarry. There is an infuriating monotony because they always go wrong 'in the same old way'. Emotional reactions with a strangely familiar all-or-nothing strength to them erupt into his attempts to manage his affairs sensibly.

As I focus upon him or her, in the middle-distance, discerning the patterns of response and tied reaction, I discern through the long-distance lens, from what he has told me, or from what my experience leads me provisionally to infer, the likely origin of these stereotyped defeats in living. The connections still have to be checked. My guess may be right or wrong as to its particular applicability. But a secure knowledge of personality theory and of the mind's defences leaves me in no doubt that bifocals are necessary wherever the old and the new are confused, as they are in people who become depressed, or who suffer from phobic anxiety or intractable personality disorders.

Is there need for an additional complication of trifocal lenses? There is, because the counsellor needs to have a third lens that focuses very close in; so close as to be able to pick up his or her own intimate responses from every part of him or herself. These reports must include all the subtle bodily changes, the emotional surges or flattenings, as my own complex personality follows the other person's story. This close-in search causes me to link up associated areas with relevant information that I have read, or to pick up similarities to and dissimilarities from other people with whom I have worked. And the inner eye makes available our spiritual discernment, whether it arises from accumulated experience, or as a specific gift of the Holy Spirit.

This moment, when the listener is facing into the same abyss of failure as the speaker, or is up against a similar block in his attempts to think through to a successful way out, for himself as well as for the other person, is a kind of impasse. How do we cope with this in our pastoral counselling? For this impasse has some characteristics which are common to all situations of deep dialogue, and some which are unique to us in particular.

All counselling situations bring out the invariable need for the helper to be empathetic, respectful and genuine. They require of us the ability to confront ourself and the other person about any significant discrepancies of mood or fact in our behaviour, within a somewhat threatened but well-maintained relationship. The sixth cardinal asset in Carkhuff's six dimensions is a clear sense of 'immediacy'.[1] By immediacy I mean the ability to know what is going on between us, in the here and now, at both verbal and non-verbal levels, ostensibly and actually. Wherever the dialogue or the mood turns, it is our task to be alongside, and to remain alongside. There

[1] R. R Carkhuff, *Helping and Human Relations*. New York, Rinehart and Winston, 1969.

are limits to the capacity of the best of us to do this, to provide what one might call a 'perilous paraklesis'.

Paraklesis or Advocacy

'Paraklesis' provides an important concept which comes from the New Testament. The word stands for the action of one who has been 'called alongside' to help, like an advocate. He finds words for us when we cannot find words for ourselves to answer our own inner or outer accusers. He 'stands alongside' and accepts the responsible task of keeping the defence moving until it 'rests' successfully against all the prosecution can do to destroy our self-esteem. This has more than passing theological links. In Christian faith, God is revealed in the person and passion of his Son as on our side, welcoming not blaming. He is alongside us whenever we fall or fail and are accused, justly or unjustly, of culpable failure. If he is there sustaining us when we have done wrong, he is all the more present when we feel that our very existence is a mistake. The role of the third person of the Trinity, the Holy Spirit, is not to draw attention to himself but to make this advocacy, representation and mediation of Christ, in the face of our accusers, a settled fact of our experience. It is because the Holy Spirit's work is to 'come alongside' us that he has traditionally been called 'the Paraclete'. He communicates to us in our personal history the eternal cosmic work of Christ as the Servant of God. 'Holiness' to judge from the actions of 'the Holy One of Israel', in Isaiah and the Psalms, is precisely that quality in God which is predictably present alongside the broken, the oppressed, the imprisoned and the desperately needy. We have twisted 'holiness' to mean almost the opposite qualities, of distance and unapproachableness.

As to being 'perilous', it was Christ who first faced this danger fully on our behalf. Part of this peril, its worst part, was to be totally identified with the 'sickness unto death'. We may think that despair, darkness and desolation are rare, until longer and deeper insearch into human beings convinces us that it is indeed universal. A despair to the point of longing for death comes to innocent children in a family of neglectful parents, sinning and sinned against in a sinful society. These children, when they come to years of discretion will, in spite of resolves to the contrary, in some way or other repeat the pattern of indiscretion, bringing darkness, desolation and death to others, as well as, perhaps, to themselves. Along with their record of earnest attempts to behave constructively, the backlog of dark guilt disturbs their moral equilibrium.

It is a matter of painful and often baffling experience that whatever is going on in the client tends to be transferred to the counsellor. How else can the sufferer really show his would-be helper what his condition feels like than by off-loading his dilemma realistically on to the man or woman who has offered to explore some way out? If the sufferer has received no answers, but only painful silence, when he has begged for help and understanding from his parents, he will tend to subject the helper to exactly the same kind of 'unhelpful' silence when he is setting up his inquiry. What seems at first 'unhelpful' can be, if we read this riddle aright, a helpful and clear entry into the central problem. How does one cope with people who will not answer? The sufferer is, perhaps unknown to himself, showing us exactly where the centre point of our empathy must be applied. We need to stay close to the uses and abuses of silence.

This is why we say that empathy needs to be accurate. For Ezekiel at Tel Aviv, sitting with the captives, it meant 'I sat where they sat'. After seven days of silence, the silence became a dialogue. The 'I' changed to a 'we'. 'We were astonished, bewildered [or as the Scots had it, "dumfoundered"] together' (Ezek. 3:15). Ezekiel's genuineness left him no other option than respectful, shared silence. His response modelled the predicament of God, as well as that of an honest assessor of a disastrous human situation. A way out would eventually be found, but it could not be seen from this vantage point. When it came it was to be a perilous road for God himself, and will be perilous for everyone who, as a vicarious, intermediary person, becomes involved in serious parakletic dialogue. Pastoral counselling is nothing less than this.

So there are general hazards, inevitable because of our shared limitations in providing the essential ingredients to deep counselling. There are also those particular snags which arise out of our individual quirks, hang-ups, areas of immaturity, unsolved emotional conflicts, hidden skeletons, temporary wild enthusiasms, permanent blind-spots, character defects, besetting sins, unrecognized fears, mechanisms of irrational flight and our own unique defensive posturing in the presence of any kind of threat, whether this takes the form of attack, smooth compliance, or a mixture of these to suit ourselves. From many years of supervising counsellors and being supervised, I know these counsellor-based distortions are of common occurence, though the precise nature of the misperception is unique to the individual.

'Attend to thyself and to the teaching, to the doctrine, to that message which is ours to teach' (I Tim. 4:16). So Paul wrote to young Timothy in charge of a difficult church situation. The wisdom required of him is to be gained by first paying attention to himself. He must ask himself what is his own essential dynamic relation to his resources on every level. What are his own initiatives and responses in behaviour, as a leader, a brother, a servant of the servants of God? How closely does the dynamic input and output of his pastoral functioning correspond to the Christ-centred model? Are the marks of Christ's perilous life-pattern being reproduced in his young apostle? 'As he is, so are we in this world' (I John 4:17 R.S.V.). The young Timothy is also a 'son of God' whose mission is liable to be misunderstood, whose powers will be envied, whose honesty will incur hatred. His love will be derided. His pursuit and punishment will become 'a public duty'. His anguish on behalf of others will arouse mockery not gratitude. The counselling contract protects the Christian pastoral counsellor from much of the hostility which ought, unless the Lord himself was mistaken, to be coming our way. However, the 'witnessing', 'admonishing', 'prophetic' and 'watch and warn' aspects of pastoral care are unsure of a welcome even from the faithful.

Attend to the Truth

Centuries of easy-going churchmanship have stereotyped pastoral care-givers as providers of 'Tender Loving Care', a non-confronting client-centredness which invites the counsellor to collude in a moral muddle. Images of boundless acceptance and limitless tolerance seem to have priority. There are certain blessed parental archetypes which come to the surface and parsons are expected to actualize them. The assumption is that pastoral care givers must wear the mantle of this wholly reassuring inclusiveness. This is an insecure assumption which leads to questionable ethics.

'Attending to himself' and 'attending to the truth he is responsible to teach' are inextricable, because the care-giver must embody the truth he teaches. This is no academic pursuit. The man must be, in a root sense, an 'amateur'. He must love the truth he pursues for the good that it does him and the deliverance it brings to others. There is a time to be silent, a time to be selective, and a time to declare 'the whole counsel of God'. Which of these appointed times is upon us waits for our sense of *kairos*. Here we need the conjunction of personal intuition, sound knowledge, training and experience, with that humility which overrides all these and enables us to listen afresh to the Holy Spirit.

The climate of counselling, of pastoral counselling as much as the secular form, implies, on the whole, an atmosphere of permissiveness. In one sense, of course, it must be so. The Gospel demands that we permit people to tell us anything about themselves without their risking our rejection of them. As Christ met us, and knowing all, made common cause with us, we in him meet others. He allowed our anger to be put on to him. He allows our defiance to exclude him from the Father he had always lovingly obeyed. He drew our just condemnation upon himself, our despair into his own heart. God in Christ permits us to come to him whatever our state; indeed, he calls us to come and from that point takes upon himself the task of putting us right. We cannot be less than this to others. In this sense, we are, or hope to be, permissive with no limits to our acceptance.

Counselling, like marriage, is based on Christ's love for the Church. It is a covenant based, not on the attractiveness of the other, but on the love of God. That love requires of us what he first gives to us. As he loves us, so we love our neighbour, which we can do in the power he gives. The love we need is covenanted love based on God as lover. Less than that is fastidiousness, 'I could love you if only . . .'. The Lord's covenant love to Peter did not retreat from the covenant into fastidiousness. He did not say 'Oh Peter, if only you hadn't betrayed me!' The covenant of the counselling offer and contract must, I believe, have something of the irresistible forward momentum and ongoingness of Christ's covenant loving. It is engaged, for better or worse, in sickness and in health, and although this makes us vulnerable, is anything less than this the love of neighbour which God both commands and enables?

But some counsellors have been, I think, seduced by the myth of a kind of pseudo-scientific objectivity. They strain after an ideal of value-free interaction with the counsellee. They believe that we can and ought to be ethically indifferent to the moral or immoral actions of our clients. If we are thinking of the client's past, the adoption of this neutral standpoint may look quite like Christ's and the Christian's unconditional welcome to the broken sufferer or returning sinner alike. But in the pastoral context this usually implies a turning away on their part from past wickedness, with a desire for something better. We do not expect to be asked to remain so ethically neutral, so 'client-centred', as to lose our own identity. If, on account of our passive listening, we are made accomplices of high-handed intentions on the part of the client to continue in a life that wilfully plans to damage others, we are acting irresponsibly. It is unrealistic to be so 'objective' as to pass over an issue without comment, on occasions when silence or 'ethical neutrality' can be construed only as compliance and agreement.

R. R. Carkhuff, whose counselling manuals are the most scientifically validated attempts so far to set the effectiveness of our activities on a sound basis, is nowhere positive about Christian faith or religion. Yet he speaks of the sheer unreality of the relationship in which the counsellor is too hide-bound by a false permissiveness to confront the other in a sensitive way, as a matter of fact, on certain occasions. There are times when the failure to point up discrepancies, with sensitive confrontation, is the mark of the ineffective counsellor. In a concerned and sensitive way, we can help the client when we draw attention to discrepancies between his ideal self-image and what he is telling us he is actually doing; discrepancies between what he puts into words about himself and what is observable by the counsellor and others from his actual behaviour, reported or present; and also between the way in which the counsellor experiences him and his actions, and the way he experiences himself. Carkhuff says, 'I respect honesty and work.'[2] He does not allow the client unrealistically to assume that he is a 'push-over', that he will let pass without comment what both recognize as dishonesty or a determined refusal to work. Without blaming, and without apologizing, this confrontation, which in other contexts could be negative and objectionable feedback, becomes an intrinsic part of effective, realistic and helpful counselling.

[2] R. R Carkhuff, *Helping and Human Relations*. New York, Rinehart and Winston, 1969.

Ethics in Counselling

It follows from what I have said that the counsellor has to attend to ethical problems in a number of separate persons and on a number of distinct levels.

1 He must attend to the ethical problem of the other person, the 'oughts' of past and present that jostle for the ear of his conscience. How does his conscience function? Is he burdened by scruples, hemmed in by chronic guilt feelings? Or does he suffer from a psychopathic inability ever to feel any compunction?

2 He will need to attend to and learn a very great deal about the expectations of this person's parents, moulding his behaviour as a baby, a child and an adult. As he walks about with his parents, and indeed their parents, inside him, his conflicts are often accounted for only by the cacophony of their discordant voices still clamouring to be heard.

3 He attends to the expectations of the social group in which the other person moved as a child, at school, in adolescence, and in which he moves throughout life. It is from social groups that the individual normally gains self-esteem by accepting the 'do's' and 'dont's' which are current at the time. When we examine the levels of ethical determination, we recognize how wide is the discrepancy between the requirements of the social groups within which a person may move every day of his life.

Identification with Modern Ethical Thinking.

In criticizing Teilhard de Chardin, Dietrich von Hildebrand takes him to task for reducing the antithesis between good and evil to mere stages of evolution, to mere degrees of perfection, ignoring the critical importance of the moral question.[3] 'In Teilhard the entire drama of man's existence, the fight between good and evil in his soul, is ignored – or, rather, overshadowed – by the evolutionary growth toward the Omega. Teilhard time and again argues that we can no longer expect modern man, living in an industrialized world and in a scientific age to accept Christian doctrine as it has been taught for the last 2,000 years. Teilhard's new interpretation of

[3] D. von Hildebrand, *Trojan Horse in the City of God.* Chicago, Franciscan Herald Press, 1967, p. 236.

Christianity is fashioned by asking, 'What fits in to our modern world?'

Von Hildebrand insists that, 'man always remains essentially the same with regard to his moral dangers, his moral obligations, his need of redemption, and the true sources of his happiness'. He sees Teilhard as falling into 'the catastrophic error of historical relativism, which confuses the socio-historical aliveness of an idea with its validity and truth'.[4]

The Church is often expected to veer in the direction of popular opinion. The winds of change blow hard against holiness and strongly for relaxed situational ethics. The Church would serve the cause of moral truth better if, like a weather vane, it pointed directly into the wind to oppose them. The question of whether a moral issue fits into the mentality of an epoch is always irrelevant, and particularly so in a time of manifest bravado in breaking down moral barriers.

Towards the end of his second letter to Timothy, the prophetic spirit of the Apostle is moved to predict that: 'The time is coming when people will not endure sound teaching, but, having itching ears, they will accumulate for themselves teachers to suit their own likings, and will turn away from listening to the truth and wander into myths' (2 Tim. 4:3–4 R.S.V.). Ours is not the first epoch to strain to fulfil that prophecy, and there may well be more to follow. To fulfil the counselling ministry like any other, the requirement is, as mentioned in Paul's next verse, 'Always be steady, endure suffering' (2 Tim. 4:5 R.S.V.).

Identification With Our Trainers

There exists, for counsellors, at times, a conflict between what we are actually aware of in ourselves and what we have been taught ought to be there. We have spoken of possible feelings of moral failure and personal guilt in the counsellor if he has yielded to the spirit of the age and compromised on some issue where the sound teaching he actually accepts, speaks otherwise. But 'the teaching' does not only derive from historic norms. It is imbibed during counsellor education with its pervasive 'do's' and 'dont's', the 'ought nevers' and 'ought always' of enthusiastic trainers. This can be

[4] Ibid., p. 237.

particularly burdensome when what is really a counselling skill has subtly become an emotional requirement. Students can be made to feel that they ought always, with every client, to feel warm, genuine, respectful, caring, friendly and even, in a professional way, loving. Is this possible when strangers troop into an agency every hour? This difficulty is particularly acute for students trained by a model suitable for long-term counselling when the agency that employs them has in mind short-term encounters, with drop-in clients who may come only once, and where long-term commitments are discouraged. Charles Warnath recently fired a salvo of protest about this:

> ... idealistic counselors-in-training are 'set-up' for later feelings of inadequacy by those counselor educators and the counseling literature that imply that effective counseling cannot occur unless counselors can respond authentically from a positive feeling toward all clients and their problems. When counselors are confronted by clients to whom they cannot respond positively, it has been my experience that they feel somewhat deficient as professionals.
>
> Phoniness in counseling does not result from a counselor's inability to respond in a genuine manner to each client, but rather from the counselor's denial that counseling relationships are susceptible to the same range of human emotions that affect any relationship between people. There is nothing inherent in the counseling situation that prevents the counselor from experiencing neutral or negative feelings, which he or she might experience toward any stranger. To deny that these emotions may exist is phony.[5]

This quotation illustrates a hidden but vital issue distinguishing Christian pastoral counselling and its best humanistic counterparts, from pseudo-religious counselling. The worst kind of 'double-bind' is suffered by those whose 'oughts for the counsellor' come from religion or from pseudo-religion. Instead of coming from the outflow of the continual love of God, with its infused, indwelling, unforced and ample graciousness to the neighbour, it becomes instead a forced, extractive effort to win approval by fidelity to the prescribed and correct feelings. This is a strained performance to gain the

[5] C. F. Warnath, 'Relationship and Growth Theories, and Agency Counselling', in *Counselor Education and Supervision*, (vol. XVII, No. 2, December 1977)) pp. 84–91.

client's approval, or, more likely, to win the approval of the moti-
vating or employing authorities.

Pseudo-religions do much the same. The more fervent training
centres in the United States for school, college, and pastoral counsellors have at times slipped into this rut. The stereotype of the
trainer has become so fixed a model, with facilitating rewards for
likeness to him and inhibiting threats to deviationists, that 'Attend
to thyself and the teaching' has become almost behaviouristic in its
rigid application. Guilt attends the attempt to adopt an individual
response, even when later work, in a different kind of agency,
invalidates the style originally taught. Professor Warnath's observations are warranted.

Both these, the religious and the pseudo-religious, put an impossible bind on their students. It is fair enough to insist that
right-standing in the counselling role requires that we act in the
manner expected from skilled and trained professionals. But to
extend this requirement and expect the same performance where
the feelings and the emotions of the heart are in question, is not
only unfair, but also implies a kind of ethical blindness to which
idealistic instructors are particularly prone. It is impossible to produce the fruits of the Spirit, love, joy, peace, patience, kindness,
goodness, faithfulness, gentleness and self-control, to order, by some
act of the will. The result in both cases is ethical double-mindedness,
more unkindly called hypocrisy. I can vouch for this in religious
counsellors as Professor Warnath does for the pseudo-religious.
They are driven to dissemble. They are scared at the contrary,
disordered emotions that surge within them. They dare not admit
these discordant feelings to others, scarcely even to themselves. Out
of fear, they produce mock emotions, pseudo-feelings and gestures
empty of 'gut' feelings. They say they feel what they ought to feel.
To mouth the required sentiments becomes the necessary substitute
for feeling them.

The law, and attempts to live by it in order to gain approval,
produce, as St Paul warned, a disastrous division in the heart of
man, leading inevitably to moral death. If we try to justify ourselves
before God or man, by struggling to act as we 'ought' to, Paul says
of us, 'You have automatically cut yourself off from Christ, you
have put yourself beyond the reach of his grace' (Gal. 5:4). This is
to move in total opposition to the Christian dynamic, which begins
by abiding in the source of life and the source of love. As Christian

counsellors we can attend to ourselves, to what we have been taught, and to our clients, only when we attend to the basic facts of our existence.

CHAPTER 6

Personal Authenticity in a Changing World

The pastoral counsellor is often dealing with people who stick out from their social background. This emerges as you study people in the context of their family setting, carefully refraining from accepting the assumption to which you are being pressured, that the one whom the family has nominated as 'the patient' is actually the sick one. Getting to know them all well can convince you that this so-called 'patient' is certainly the least sick. In a family so emotionally flat-chested, he or she is the only one who ever attempted to stick the chest out. The rest scarcely breathe.

For example, even when she was a child the family could not stand Dora's comments. They were naïve, but so penetrating that they raised intolerable questions of emotional fact. Her family (as families often do) kept up a verbal fiction as to how close, loving, united and ideal they were. But no stone was ever turned to see what lay underneath this 'sales-talk'. Words with no backing of emotional reality had devalued the domestic currency of communication. The only one to notice this and blurt it out was Dora. So she became 'the patient'. In due course, invalidated and confused, clinging to her version of 'truth', she was taken to a psychiatrist as a child, and again in adolescence. They complained that she wouldn't 'fit in'. She was always 'the odd one out'. She could not have 'fallen into line' unless first she had betrayed her own perceptions of reality and sold out to that overwhelming majority.

To be truthful and authentic was what mattered most in Dora's life. To 'fit in' with that family would have been to commit moral and mental suicide. Eventually she left home feeling still homeless. Even when away from the family, the verbal clatter persisted in her ears. In the loneliness that inevitably followed her leaving the family that had never been a family for her, and without the social confidence to make friends, a crescendo of their old condemnations led to even deeper self-rejection. She suffered the agoraphobia of aloneness and the claustrophobia of shut-in-ness. She still felt surrounded by a hostility from which escape was impossible. This led to a despairing sense of such badness, every way she turned, that at times she longed for death.

The emotionally sick family may nominate, as the blameworthy sick one, either the ugly duckling who is really a swan, or the ugly duckling who is really the ugliest duckling. The choice of the scapegoat falls upon the one who 'sticks out' – that is the crucial factor. This factor determined both the demand that Jesus be crucified for being too good, and the thieves on each side of him for being too bad.

'Standing-out' is a factor that commonly puts people under such pressure that they feel abnormal. They are under duress to comply with the weight of social opinion, even at the expense of their own integrity. If something in the individual rebels against the weight of group opinion, the person with a strong, independent, confident ego or self will maintain his or her own stance. Quite appropriately, he asserts his right to be different. The 'leader', for this is what he has become, may or may not be conscious that he is appealing away from the customs and morals of the community around him to an 'ethical absolute'. There is an inescapable ethical preference which has grasped him. He becomes the bearer of a better expression of man's duty to man and a challenge to the group to accept their need for ethical development towards caring and responsibility. All our great social reformers, so many of whom have been 'outstanding' men and women, have done this. They have been attacked for doing it, often for many years, before the advance which began with their lonely stand was recognized.

A person with a weaker and less secure ego can be just as right as the strong person in his or her discontent with the low standards their group accepts. A smaller natural endowment of self-assurance and confidence is compatible, but not comfortable, with being equally offended at the uncaring customs of the herd around you. In outstandingly courageous people it is a splendid synthesis of potentiality and ability. In weaker personalities their very strengths tear them apart. A strong and accurate critical perception is apt to be abrasive. Its possessor is seldom comfortable.

A society does not have to be decadent to be one in which the ethically outstanding person is made to stand out painfully. The individual may just be out of step, historically, with the developmental age of the group whose authority gives them the right to make ethical decisions on behalf of others. In 1908 the Lambeth conference of bishops of the Anglican Church condemned contraception (other than by the unsafe 'safe-period') as 'demoralizing to character and hostile to national welfare'. Fifty years later, in 1958, the same episcopal conference classified the use of contraception in the planning of a family and the enjoyment of intercourse within marriage (without fear, therefore, of an unwanted pregnancy) as 'sacred duties'.

Who is to say whether the bishops' 1908 pronouncement, or their contradiction of it in 1958 is closer to the mind of the Spirit who is constantly guiding the Church into the whole truth? What is disturbing, from the pastoral counselling angle, is the tendency for ecclesiastical opinion to reflect a pale and belated recognition of a change in secular public opinion. We want to ask what happened to those individuals who, in 1908, were the bearers of the prophetic word about freeing marriage from so much fear and adding to it so much joy – supposing the 1958 decision to represent 'the mind of Christ' for Christians. I have counselled people for the past twenty-five years who were born, as I was, in the decade after 1908. Our ethical standards, very firmly imprinted by religiously conscientious parents who heeded their Edwardian bishops, have never permitted us to feel comfortable about contraception. I meet couples nowadays, twenty to forty years our juniors, still in the child-bearing years, who are bewildered by the contradictory voices that press upon them, from the media, the manufacturers, the Mothers' Union, the Marriage Guidance Council, the neighbours, from their own private thoughts and from conversations with a spouse. He or she may be equally baffled or, denying there is a problem, press the other partner urgently to conform with whatever he or she chooses to regard as 'the done thing'.

Too many life-decisions are undergoing ethical transition. This can be so troublesome as to precipitate breakdown in over-pressurized people who have a firm conscience of their own but not much independent strength. These conflicts include the whole area of sexual ethics. People are worried enough to lose sleep and slide into anxiety depressions with which they come for help, over such debated issues as intercourse before and outside marriage, same-sex intercourse, divorce and remarriage, sexual deviations, abortions, sterilization and a combination of these now apparently *sub judice* matters. Whatever course of action they decide upon, some influential person or persons will disapprove. Depending as they do for self-esteem on approval of their actions, they pick up, and pick upon, the disapprovals. Chronic guilt and self-blame are their constant companions. They need a rest from this destructive self-punishment and deliverance from its subtle pay-offs. They need to hear Mother Julian's: 'I saw no blame.'

The pastoral counsellor is not, I think, finally answerable to curial or episcopal authority, particularly at a time when today's pronouncement may be overturned tomorrow. It seems to be our task to enable the person to hear the 'still, small voice' within themselves, and to strengthen their ability to stand by the *faith* that is in them (Rom. 11:20). The principle I hold to is, 'whatsoever is not of faith, is sin' (Rom. 14:23 A.V). However, because 'there is a way which seems right to a man but its end is the way to death' (Prov. 14:12 R.S.V), we need collateral checks from all the authorities a person respects and we respect. In giving pastoral care we work with the other to find and to clarify good reasons, soundly based on the Word of God and the Wisdom of the Spirit for behaving one way and not otherwise. The New Testament norm is that this should be conveyed by, and converge in, the intimate group of like-minded believers. But it may be that the client is at odds with his or her support group. He demands of the counsellor more space, more silence, and more assistance in formulating his own convictions than the group has allowed.

I would like to dispose of the possible accusation that this determination on the part of the counsellor, to permit the client to discover his or her own conscience, and the reasons that lead to specific convictions, is disloyal to the Church authorities who, often enough, have entrusted people to his care. Roman Catholic readers will recognize that this determination to pay close attention to the individual voice of conscience is in the tradition of the Second Vatican Council. The responsible Catholic theologian Fr Bernard Häring, writes:

It is a fundamental principle of Christian ethics that man has to follow the judgment of his conscience, even when it is in error. ... No one has a monopoly on truth; not even the magisterium of the Catholic Church makes a distinctionless claim to such a monopoly for itself. ...

It staggers the imagination to think that an earthly authority or an ecclesiastical magisterium could take away from man his own decision of conscience... Each man views the world in a special way; each has special opportunities for watching over particular values and duties, especially those that correspond to his place in history. Only deference to everyone's conscience and fidelity to one's own conscience make it possible to realize the world of moral values in all its richness ... The church is deeply concerned about the unity of all men in faith. But it is precisely this concern that forbids her to do anything that would be detrimental to conscience.[1]

Sometimes 'pastoral counsellors', who owe much to their training in psycho-dynamics, come under criticism from 'spiritual directors' in the Catholic tradition (more from the Anglican than the Roman). The brunt of the criticism lies in the charge that they are too subjective, not solidly based on the wisdom of the past, careless of canon law and of the casuistry or case-law ('casuistry' is not always to be used pejoratively) which was built up by the great Catholic directors of the eighteen and nineteenth centuries. From the Protestant side there are criticisms that they are not soundly based in the unchanging moral principles of Puritanism (which again, for me, is basically a 'good' word). From both, it is said that they lack prudence in relation to the past and the firm decisions on what is right and wrong for Christians. These are meant to be crushing criticisms, invalidating a 'too subjective' approach. We are put in a tight corner by the moral criteria of past ages.

Prudence

As one who for some years has given a regular course of lectures at a theological college on the history of pastoral care, my mind and heart have subjected themselves to those stern old pastors of the Church in former ages. But what is prudence, that 'virtue' so sought

[1] B. Häring, *The Christian Existentialist* (University of London Press). p. 6.

after by spiritual counsellors in their careful direction of souls? Bernard Häring has opened up for me a view of prudence which has rescued it from the stolid and vaguely stodgy, to a new concept which I find exciting, timely, original, relevant, dynamic and innovative.

Häring acknowledges the narrow horizon of past attempts to systematize the 'moral theology' which lies at the basis of pastoral counselling.

> Unfortunately, current manuals of moral theology, reflecting Catholic moral theology of the last two centuries, fail to portray the riches of the community of salvation and salvific history of hope. This holds true also for the virtue of prudence, which may be defined as the act of adapting our action to the redemptive actions of Christ within the whole history of salvation and in the context of a present salvific community.[2]

He contrasts the old, static, codified case-law approach with that of the new theology, with its authentic, biblical determination to start both where people are in the world today, and with the faith once delivered to the saints. This means to proceed by passing back and forth from the one to the other. The overriding concern is to be real to people and real to the living Christ, our contemporary. The Holy Spirit proceeds from one Person of the Trinity to the other, from God to us, and from us to God, and between ourselves. He is the daily renewing co-inherent enabler of this core task of every theologian (in the sense that all God's people are theologians) conveying God's word back and forth effectively, where time and eternity are conjoined.

Pastoral counselling is pre-eminently concerned with enabling people to do the right thing at the right time. It makes the actively active task possible. It is equally important to facilitate the actively passive task which is, when the occasion is favourable, to make it possible to assimilate into consciousness those experiences of early infantile and childhood pain which, until this favourable moment, have necessarily and prudently been shut away. The inherent wisdom of the psyche has insisted on its dissociation and defence by repression. Abundant health, both within the person and in the environment and occasion provided by the group, creates a favour-

2 Ibid., p. 70.

able possibility for a deliberate breakthrough, dissolving those defences so that integration can take place. To help people to do, or to bear (a kind of not doing), whatever constitutes the probable next stage of growth and development, at the most favourable, or the least unfavourable time, is a focal task of pastoral counselling.

Timing

This concept is precisely contained in the important New Testament Greek term *kairos*. It means the favourable moment, the right moment, the appropriate opening of a door at the time when it is right to walk through it, or the closing of a door when it ought to be closed. Jesus Christ had a brilliantly clear sense of *kairos* and frequently shared this awareness of his with the disciples. Can we, as counsellors, be endowed by his Spirit with his impeccable sense of the right time?

Some of the saddest and most frustrating moments in counselling are those when we stand by helpless while earnest and well-meaning people make a muddle of their timing. They have never since birth been able to get their timing right. When an obviously open door invites them to enter they are hesitant. Some indefinable fear of hidden consequences inhibits them. Their sensible advisers urge them to act at once, because the time and the occasion seem to them to be obviously right, and ripe for the taking. But they are seized by a compulsion to delay, which is more powerful than all the persuasions of reason which urge immediate action. And then, when the door has closed, with monotonous repetitiveness they know with entire certainty that they have missed the favourable moment. The *kairos* has passed.

There is sometimes detectable, alongside their disappointment, a certain grim satisfaction that this proves again that life has done the dirty on them, so somehow they have 'won'. At least they were not going to be conned into taking a decision under pressure, to go through a certain door into an unknown and almost certainly worse future. Their satisfaction is not unlike that of the workman who refused to obey the safety regulations in respect of some scaffolding. Predictably, the time came when he fell to the ground and broke his back. As they were carrying him away he was heard to mutter, 'Well, at least I showed them I couldn't be bossed.'

This frustrating, compulsive behaviour often yields dramatically to peri-natal primal work. The inhibited individual discovers that the door he is refusing to be pressured to go through has become likened in his mind to the pelvic outlet, and the whole process has become confused with his own birth. The door at the exit of the birth passages did lead to a worse experience, perhaps that of a mind-shattering isolation or some other bad post-natal experience. The imprinted memory of the occasion includes a promise, made at the time, that he or she would never undergo it again for anyone. Hence the satisfaction he finds in his delaying tactics. At the peri-natal level he is wisely preferring the pressured, yet safe, surrounding holding of the passages on this side of the door. By doing this he is defeating those who, according to his feelings at the primal level, would like to push him out into the enormities of an expanding cosmos in which everything that could be helpful receded into infinity and left him in a lonely hell.

Even in relation to peri-natal events he was out of step with *kairos*. It was indeed the right time to be born. But he is convinced that this stubborn refusal is protecting him against a repetition of the pain that accompanied the first occasion when he let himself be pushed through that door. To the infant mind, that experience beyond the door was, and still is, unbearable as well as incomprehensible. Now, in a supportive adult group, having understood in general the task to be undertaken, he can, with full comprehension, let the whole process happen again. He relives both the birth, which he recognizes as passing through the door, and the absolute loneliness beyond it, which for the first time, though sufficiently terrifying, becomes bearable. Thereafter he will have no need to foul his timing mechanism by getting today's doors of opportunity mixed up with the primal doors.

For the Christian the 'right time', *kairos*, is of fundamental importance. Christ came as Son of God among man, at a time determined by the Father, whose redemptive plan was being put into action in history. Throughout his life, Christ was totally turned towards the Father, listening to him with perfect obedience, to receive from him that perfect sense of timing for every word he said and every act he performed. This total correspondence of task and occasion constitute his perfect life of limitation. He does nothing out of time, he says nothing out of place. Seven times in St John's Gospel we hear the positive statement, 'I do what the Father has for me to do or say.' Fourteen times we hear from Christ the negative or limiting counterpart. 'I say . . ..do . . . nothing except what my Father has for me . . .'. to do, or say.

The average Christian is content to get the general drift of what it seems God intends him to be doing, and then proceeds, *ad lib*, to stride or dawdle along the same road. The notion that every moment needs to be a moment of watchfulness, prayerfulness and attentiveness is no part of his life concept. He has absolutely no sense of *kairos* unless, like Christian upon the Pilgrim Road, he meets someone else with definite ideas of what is the right time and what he should be doing.

When everybody else had gone up to the feast of Tabernacles in Jerusalem, and certainly expected Jesus to be with them, he deliberately stayed behind. He meant to go, but he did not do the obvious and go with the others. He contrasts here his attitude towards *kairos* with that of the family for whom the common customs were a sufficient guide to conduct. Christ says, 'My time has not yet come: but your time is always ready (John 7:6 A.V.). One of the translations has it, 'Anytime is good enough for you. . . . Go to the feast, I am not going yet because my time is not yet fulfilled' (John 7:6,8).

In the discourses within the last week of his life, Christ shares his sense of *kairos* or the almost equivalent word *hora*, his hour. At Cana, at the marriage feast, when his mother urged him to act as soon as the wine ran short, perhaps in order to avoid embarrassment, his answer is, 'My hour has not yet come' (John 2:4 R.S.V.). Before that astonishing sacrament in which Jesus Christ washed his disciples' feet, John writes in his Gospel: 'Jesus knew that his hour had come to depart out of this world to the Father, having loved his own who were in the world, he loved them to the end' (John 13:1 R.S.V.).

In the garden of the agony, Jesus prayed, 'What shall I say? Father, deliver me from this hour? It is for this hour that I have come. Father glorify your name' (John 12:27). This refers back to the occasion when his divinely appointed limit ('I am not sent but unto the lost sheep of the house of Israel' — Matt. 15:24 A.V.) seemed likely to be overstepped by the request of some Greeks to see him and he replied: 'The hour has come in which the Son of man is glorified. Verily, I say to you, unless a grain of wheat fall into the ground and die, it remains alone. But if it die, it brings forth much fruit' (John 12:23).

As Christ was, so it is our wisdom to be in the world, constantly alert to *kairos*. All our spiritual senses, the metaphysical counterparts so to speak, of sight, hearing, smell, taste and touch, can be alive to the possibility that the Holy Spirit will use any one of them to indicate some change of direction, to halt, or to move forward at once, a voice behind saying, 'This is the way, walk in it.'

It is my experience that people who come for counselling are usually at a point of significant transition. A significant moment of time, a *kairos* is upon them. Or they have missed the right occasion, and are bewildered as to how to get back on the road. This call to be present alongside others at the moment of *kairos*, aware of its infinite significance, anxious as to how they use the time and the choice they make, this call constitutes the weightiest responsibility for the pastoral counsellor.

This strong sense of *kairos* must, on occasion, come into conflict with the very natural desire men and women have to live in safety, and in compliance with codified customs, expected responses, social convention, ecclesiastical patterning, denominational conformity and all the other things we do to keep in line. There are implicit guarantees to individuals given by society, that if you observe our way of life, we on our part will guarantee to sustain your self-esteem. You will not lose face among us. Homogeneous social groups – such as middle-class congregations usually are – seldom fail to demonstrate that well-known sociological law by which pressure is put upon deviants, those above the line or those below it, those who want to be better or turn out to be worse. Both are pushed inwards towards the middle position, mediocre though that may be. The threat is withdrawn when the waywardness is curtailed, by signs that the deviator is now willing to live within the accepted behavioural limits. Stable societies of this kind expect their leaders to show the anger and impatience they all feel with the irritating eccentrics who go off at a tangent. What right have they to claim that God is calling them, not to carry on as before, but to do that which is different from the tradition? Yet my conviction is that the counsellor who is unaware of this possibility, that authenticity may mean standing out against the social norm, cannot fail to do great disservice to Christian people, should he be called upon to counsel them.

In concluding this chapter, let me return briefly to the word 'prudence' in relation to *kairos*. Bernard Häring writes:

Christian prudence is the action of love that hopes, of a love that strives with all its strength for the goal, in keeping with the demands of the living reality.

Prudence . . . consists more in the humble awareness of God's loving and wise providence than in self-sufficient planning.

The virtue of prudence helps the individual discover his uniquely personal response to the challenges and opportunities of his existence.[3]

Such definitions help us towards such a theological and dynamic understanding of decision-making in pastoral care.

[3] Ibid., pp. 70–3.

CHAPTER 7

Christian Problems with Anger and Negative Feelings

Feeling Angry – A Good Achievement or a Bad Fault?

There are many depressed people whose inner conflict consists in the tiring tussle between ancient rages within, fanned into smouldering anger by present-day frustrations, and the forces of fear that keep such feelings under control. They never burst into flame in consciousness because of the forceful repressive and suppressive mechanisms that control them so totally that such people will deny they are angry. Christ's comments in St John's Gospel about harbouring a lie at the heart, about guile as an obstacle to the Holy Spirit's purifying action (8:44–5) are particularly relevant to this condition.

Is it the task of pastoral care to see to the removal of this inner anger without ever allowing the person to become conscious of it, or of the persons towards whom it is keenly but surreptitiously felt? My answer to this is No! Christ has provided himself as the one who offers to take our angry blows upon himself. Hurting oneself leads to depression, self-castigation, obsessional rituals and masochistic practices, none of which is a frank or honest expression of anger. Hurting others, off-loading anger on to the weak, is not the way out.

So we help depressed people and others like them to become aware of the cauldron within and to get in touch with its primary causes and early connections. We give them opportunities to offload anger in safe and acceptable ways. The burden which has weighed them down lifts off them as they do this.

Let us look at a typical situation that a Christian can bring to the counsellor:

What has happened to make me feel so much worse as a person just at the time when God is so real to me and has been showing himself and his love for me as never before? All kinds of secret sins and shortcomings seem to be staring me in the face. That this should happen just when I have come alive spiritually in so many joyful ways does not make sense.

In particular I am at a loss to know how to deal with all the anger that seems to be welling up inside me. There is so much that is good happening in me. I don't want to sound as though I'm going backwards rather than forwards. What should I do about these contradictory directions I seem to be going in?

My answer is that coming alive to God and experiencing his goodness and love does make people more aware of 'ungodly' feelings like anger. They hoped to be able to put their anger away and feel genuinely more loving to everybody. The fact that it is so hard to share this makes them feel that anger must be something wrong and shameful. People want to know what to do with such feelings. Should they fight them down or confess them?

Let us look at the background of such people. In the years before they came to this renewed experience in Christ, there were probably times when they became depressed. They may well have reacted to disappointment or injustice, not by showing feelings openly but by going quiet, withdrawing, feeling unaccountably tired, and becoming generally low spirited but certainly without any show of anger or open resentment. Religious people, and even conscientious people who have no contact with the Church at all, are prone to depression as well as disappointment when things do not go as well as they expected. If this is the case, then the anger is the *honest* presence now of the *hidden* anger that was actually present in the depression they experienced before. Anger is present in every depressed person but it is covered up by mental defence mechanisms that can be summed up in the word 'guile'.

These mechanisms are established very early in life. Many things happen to us in babyhood that make us angry. It is not possible for parents to meet all our needs. Angry crying is the natural response. Most mothers are not threatened when their babies react to disappointment in this way. They accept it as an emotion which can be shared. It is not a pleasant feeling, but the baby can be honest about it, mother permitting. The competent mother is concerned, but not put out by the anger shown when she has to leave her baby to attend to other things for a while.

Some parents, however, cannot tolerate anger in their offspring. They feel guilty and depressed enough already and are pushed by it to the limits of their endurance. To have to listen to the angry crying of an obviously unhappy and discontented baby, when you have already done all you can think of to stop it and have tried to meet its round-the-clock needs, is too much. So an angry voice is heard, 'Oh shut up. Stop your noise, can't you? Be quiet.' This may be accompanied by an angry slap or threatening gesture to reinforce the threatening tones of the angry voice. This teaches the infant a prime lesson about life. Parents can be angry. That is their right. The baby must never be angry. So the baby splits off the anger at unmet needs and develops a placid exterior. Guile pays. It makes friends, even for babies and children. It influences people. The baby learns to hide away wrath and hopes fervently that it will never be uncovered.

The more strenuous the guile the greater the parental reward. Since at this level of experience parents are confused with God, religion which claims to speak for God gets into the bad habit of rewarding the concealment of anger which actually exists, by means of this guile.

The God of the Psalmists speaks in a totally different way. 'Blessed is the man . . . in whose spirit there is no guile' (Ps. 32:2). When we come to the New Testament we learn that the character of God is such that even violent anger in us, such as leads to the murder of his Son on the Cross, does not prevent him, in exactly the same moment that we prove that we are his murderers, from declaring that we are also his beloved.

'Father, forgive them,' he said as they drove in the nails, 'they do not know what they are doing.' It was not their own anger that the hammering hands of the soldiers expressed. It was the anger of others, particularly of the religious, that gave murderous force to the nails.

God does not accept people because they have a long and successful religious record in the guileful concealment of rage. Nor does he reject anyone when the anger stored up since infancy bursts into consciousness, as the armour of guile is shattered by the Spirit of truth.

Occasions for Splitting off Anger

This guile or concealment of an emotion which is too threatening to the infant's relationship with the all-powerful parents to be allowed to remain in consciousness, is itself the result of an internal splitting-off of real feelings. When they were split off they immediately became part of the unconscious. Behind the secondary emotion of anger and rage lies the situation of basic needs which the mother could not or did not meet. For example, if her birth passages could not relax to give the baby a fighting chance of getting through and out, then the sensations of terror could give rise to an explosive anger – which could not get out then and cannot get out now. The memory of the imprisoning walls is still there, to stop people from expressing their frustration at such unreasonable, huge, overwhelming, crushing and suffocating opposition.

Pre-natal Rage

Much earlier than in the birth, within a couple of months of conception, the foetus has had (as we showed in discussing the maternal-foetal distress syndrome) ample experience of unmet need, of rage at the injustice of it, and of restraining aggression out of sympathy for the mother. Undoubtedly this is the place where the human organism first learns to control anger at unmet needs, to protect the environment from its destructiveness, to control it forcibly or turn its force against the self. All this surging conflict is recorded in the history of early uterine life. Characteristically, when depression takes its origin here, the individual has a hypersensitive regard for the feelings of others but (as in the womb) refuses to be aware of or acknowledge any needs of his own. Yet on the deeper, repressed level, underneath layers of denial, there *is* anger, and below this an anguish of disappointment and pain of loss, and below that, an unsuspecting, hopeful foetus still holding on to its original 'shopping-list'.

A God of truth and justice must be one who himself works for the resolution of this kind of situation. It would be against his character not to provide for the reconciliation and at-one-ment of the baby-within-the-adult to these basic experiences of injustice and rage in the womb.

It will involve being born again by reliving it all, including the explosive anger, with the help of a person's presence. Christians who relive the experience, sustained by the willing entry of Christ into their afflictions, are apt to remember Christ's crown of thorns, and thank God that he knows something of what it is like. As Geoffrey Hill's *The Pentecost Castle* sums it up,

> dealing his five wounds
> so cunning and so true
> of love to rouse this death . . .

Post-natal Anger

Basic needs are not met when the mother is unable or unwilling to offer herself and her almost constant presence to the baby during the waking hours of the first weeks and months. Babies live as persons and grow in basic trust insofar as they can live in the reliable presence of the mother. It is that which builds up a sound self-hood and human being-as-a-person. Well-being and the sense of 'how good and glorious it is to be me' derive from the times the baby can spend looking up at a loving and adoring countenance. These are basic needs. It is part of the parental contract to meet these needs. If the mother does not come, the baby is pushed progressively, by loss of trust and hope, into despair, then through mounting separation-anxiety and panic towards a cliff edge. If the situation goes on too long and no one comes 'in time', there is a fall into dread, disintegration, death of the self, and nothingness. Most of our defensive flights into diversionary living take their origin from our need not to go back into or near this place of dread.

Some religious disciplines keep down the hot fires of anger (sometimes also of loving) by introducing a state of rigidity. We become what Bishop Taylor Smith used to call 'Christmas-Tree Christians'. We have no root, and no fruit. We tie attractive baubles (good works done for public admiration) on to dead branches, and are angry if they are not noticed and approved of.

The Rejection of Bad Feelings in Small Groups

Renewal changes the whole inner climate of the personality. A new miracle of spring takes place, followed by a warm growing season and the full sunshine of summer. In the winter of religion nothing grew, despite the appearances. Now everything grows, the foliage, flowers and fruits of the Spirit. But (to pursue the image) weeds grow too, since their roots and seeds, too, have been frozen hard. These can be unexpected and horrifying for the renewed Christian to see. Some may even decide to return to the more comfortable, cooler climate of 'religion' rather than risk having to declare to their prayer group or 'Christian' friends the contents of their depression, the same as everyone else's, anxiety, rage, despair and lust, with loss of joy and vitality and little energy.

Some do risk sharing the darker side of their enhanced self-awareness, hoping that the group which has been eager to share their joy will be equally willing to share their pain, or whatever else that shadow-side brings to their notice. The saddest part of my work during the past six or eight years has been having to listen to Christians who had been 'renewed in the Holy Spirit' recounting the rejection they met when they attempted to be honest about the murkier, bleaker, more ominous and obscure aspects of their inner life. These 'blots' had so baffled and harassed them as to need to be shared with someone. The 'prayer group' had seemed to be the obvious place for honest sharing, and yet they had been aware at the time of an element of risk. For months their shared experiences had been of joy and victory. They had so enjoyed being close to each other, for warmth and outgoing happiness radiated attractively across the group. The emotions they had now become aware of were not attractive, not such as a man would wish to warm himself by, but rather suggest to him that he put on an overcoat to counteract the chill. So, to speak of 'negative' feelings honestly was inevitably to break the charmed atmosphere, to hint at the existence of another world, dark and even sinister, with dire threats of being near to coming into close contact with bad feelings.

In spite of these fears, they spoke – into a silence that became increasingly uncomfortable, or into the painful experience of being silenced. Some were frankly put down and made to feel ashamed for having spoken.

When we have reflected carefully on those shattering (that is not too strong a word) rebuffs, this pattern has emerged. The member had shared honestly the dark feelings that were pressing up into his or her body, mind and spirit, like a heavy cloud obscuring the accustomed sun. There had been at once an uneasy silence in the group, waiting for the leader to deal with this unprecedented item on the agenda. After the uncomfortable silence, someone had led off on another tack altogether, making no reference at all to what had just been said, launching out, with somewhat pointed superiority, into some 'inspirational theme'. This tends to happen when I myself talk in 'charismatic' groups about the emergence of the negative under the influence of the Holy Spirit's 'spring cleaning' of the cellars of the memory. The subject is 'short-changed', my concern firmly dropped.

The effect of this 'put-down' on the anxious sharer is devastating. They feel the group life they have come to depend on and their acceptance in it are tottering on the brink of disintegration. They have shared the worst that they fear to be true of themselves and the group quite plainly did not want to know. They feel suddenly obliterated, wiped off the table of the group-life like a dirty stain, killed off as a worthwhile person. As to that essential self-esteem we gain from others, they feel evacuated and left with a nauseating empty feeling, sick at heart and hurt deep in the guts.

This is the moment when the leadership is on trial. The too honest sharer, feeling put down, looks to the leadership for support and vindication, if not for their virtue, at least for their honesty. It has never, I regret to say, for those many who have shared the experience of such groups with me, been forthcoming. If it were, it would be another kind of group altogether, whose members would not have had to bring their dark night noises for us to listen to and validate.

The leadership has a responsibility here which goes unremarked at the time but is vital to the ongoing life of the group. If, with a courage that can leave the ninety and nine in their cosy but fast-crumbling fold, he can remind the group that John or Mary has just shared a personal anguish and that so far they had, pointedly, not even acknowledged the person or the pain, but by silence tried to shame them for having spoken, then there is hope for the group, hope for renewal, hope for its ongoing Christian dynamics. In the cases I have heard of this has not been done. The sharer has felt let down by and justifiably angry with the leadership and the whole group, tending to leave that evening's meeting alone and in disgrace.

Next week there is a crisis: do I go again or do I stay away? If I do go, who is it that goes? The chastened and corrected John or Mary, resolved never again to risk being disgraced, resolved to act the cheerful charismatic cover-up to the evident satisfaction of all? But that is not the essence of renewal but of the old religion. However skilfully last week's well-shamed sharer contrives this week to smile at the group and the leader who let him down cruelly, there will be anger to be hidden. The smile comes through inwardly clenched teeth. The throat is tight, the solar plexus sore and tremulous, the heart may miss a beat and bump over the next. The whole meeting proves tiring, so much energy has to be spent on justifying the admonished self by an effort to be cheerful again, and an effort to conceal the resentment by skilful guile.

Not just for the one, but for each member of that prayer group, last week's meeting was a vital trend-setter, a notification of a new requirement, a cautionary episode. If any among them had already deliberated on taking the risk of sharing honestly and had teetered on the brink of what would have sounded like 'confession', that possibility can now be tucked away for ever. A part of each of them was grateful to the leadership for dealing so swift a death blow to the emergence of such 'morbid' and 'depressing' symptoms from one of God's 'renewed' people. But another part, the hurt child within each, alongside which the Holy Spirit had been groaning, sinks to the ground in despair. It never will be heard in this group, and if not here, nowhere and never. So everybody is now condemned to be guarded, evasive, cautious and selective about what is shared. The false-self system, as R. D. Laing called it, is put into operation, until it is not men and women who meet, but masks. The actions are more and more a kind of puppetry, nicely calculated to keep the phony group happily phony. The accustomed, safe, religious, inter-personal distances, which had been so wonderfully overcome by the Spirit of Truth in the renewal, are now back again. The closeness, and with it the sustaining quality of the group, has been lost. Why rub salt into the wound by continuing to meet when all that made meeting so soul-refreshing has departed? The unexpressed feelings of anger, resentment, disappointment and disenchantment block up the inner channels, and depression appears as a further disfigurement to be concealed. Why not return to the familiar, time-honoured distances between the well-known strangers in the pews? There discretion, a correct discreetness, has been observed for so many centuries, it is built in to being British. The National Initiative for Evangelism notes the falling numbers of Church attenders in the major denominations yet the increase in house church membership. This may well be a reflection of these tendencies. There is a famine, in an increasingly impersonal, constricted, and suspicious world, for personal salvation, for feet 'set in a large room' among trusting people.

The leaders of the Fountain Trust recently, in 'joyful obedience', closed down the operation. I cannot help feeling that if they had been genuinely open to this darker side, of the essential growth of persons in prayer groups, they would have realized that the work of training and inspiring a spiritually courageous and competent leadership has scarcely begun. That, I am sure, is the next stage if the prayer groups and house churches are to survive, their members to mature and stay open to their mission to one another's inner world, and to the outer world which is also not easily reached. Not being party to the deliberations that led to the closing of the Trust I may be way off course. Had I been present I would have pressed for its continuance with a new emphasis on the Holy Spirit's darker work, his intention to glorify Christ by reconciling us to our weak and disfigured selves. This child of the past we would rather shut away, like a plague sufferer, in quarantine. There is need for a trained and courageous eldership, delivered from its own fears of losing popularity, able to proclaim the whole counsel of God.

It was the spiritual genius of Paavo Ruotsalainen (1777–1852) the leader of the Renewal Movement in Finland, to emphasize from the start that if renewal were genuine, after the initial 'honeymoon period', for about half of those who had joined it, the early elevation of spirits and buoyancy of mood would come to an end, to be invaded, even replaced, by all manner of dark feelings and disturbing and unseemly emotions. They represented deep memories of old injuries, at the basis of the distrusts and enmities between members of the Community of Christ's Body. As such they were to be brought into the light of day and the group's love, seen to be the disordered imaginations which Christ's Kingdom overthrows and put off like old clothes, as 'the old man'. John Wesley, too, spoke of 'all hell being let loose' when the 'honeymoon period' was over.

I have a reasoned hope that the Catholic renewal groups will continue to listen to the negative, dark-night aspects of Christian growth and maturation, and develop, and what is more important, *institutionalize* that service to those who need it, and will train leaders and facilitators for it.

In India in 1968–9, conducting eighteen week-long seminars in pastoral counselling for clergy, teachers and doctors of the Church of South India, with an admixture of Roman Catholic priests, I remember the shock and almost terror of the CSI men and women that the Catholics could be so unashamedly honest about their sins and shortcomings. Those who come on our courses from renewal prayer fellowships and other church groups in England tend to come under a cloud, as individuals. Even if they benefit greatly and would like to share what has happened to them, this is frowned upon. They have been 'dabbling in psychology'. They have been 'indulging in self-pity' when in fact they have been obeying the Lord's command to let the children come to him.

They speak of the tendency for prayer groups to reach a certain point, living in close fellowship, love and shared joy, but then to fall away. As we talk about this issue, again the familiar division emerges between those, on the one hand, who are aware of the need for deeper trust, sharing and closeness, to make more painful growth crises bearable, and to evangelize the roots of our resistances to the love which will cast out our communal fears, and those on the other hand who have had bad experiences in groups that 'got too intro-spective', and sheered off depth work in people. They want to res-pond to new and expansive initiatives, seeing progress essentially in the united carrying through of active programmes, even at the risk of becoming wholly extrovert. The Devil chuckles – if he can rise to humour – when he can divide the Church between those who are strong on inner evangelism and growth and those who are strong on the outer. In effect each is justifying an area of weakness that the Evil One will contrive to make fatal for the Church's balanced growth.

Encounter groups, even Christian ones in the Catholic Marriage Encounter Movement, arouse stiff resistance in Christians who in-sist on being saved from themselves without ever first meeting themselves emotionally. The encounter groups are wary of charis-matic groups because their members do tend to avoid emotional reality and encounter as soon as they run into less pleasing channels. Some charismatics look down on encounter groups as so humanistic and horizontal, earthy and this-worldly as to have only the most tenuous dealings with the vertical dimension of grace and life in the Holy Spirit. This charge would be strongly rebutted but there is some substance to it.

Each needs the genius of the other. The prayer groups need to learn the bitter-sweet gains of honest and plain-speaking, sharing in groups, as the vehicle of the Holy Spirit's reconciliation of lost parts of the individual, helped by the group's care. Encounter groups for Catholic marrieds need a sustained sense of the priority of Christ's love of the Church as their model, not arguing from the human to the divine. They have, I know, had couples from the renewal in them, for it is they who are now open to our approach at this time.

Group Life as the Essential Context to Counselling

This consideration, in some detail, of the organizations promoting group life to various specifications is not merely relevant, but also central to the task of counselling. We are more than in a tight corner if we neglect it. We are at a dead end. The growth the individual makes in therapy is almost impossibly difficult to maintain if the family, church, or social group to which the person returns is living in ways that are totally unsympathetic to the serious task of personal insearch, to spending energy on fostering inner transformation. It is helpful in all cases and essential in some, to have as a background to any individual counselling, a supportive and genuinely human group to relate to in daily life. That is why we urge several people to come from the same church or community to be the nucleus of a group prepared to offer care in some depth and mediate its meaning to those in the community who are only averagely interested.

Counselling, if it is not to be a flash in a pan, must have an institutional, socially validated group base, growing in relational caring and skills along with the individuals who are learning to care for their own hurt child with advancing skills. The nature we have inherited, that the Creator continues to maintain and to renew, works through relationships. The whole thrust of Catholic theology and pastoralia since Vatican II has been to stress this. It is, after all, no more than a return to the focal concerns, about people's way of relating, of the Evangelists, of Paul, Peter, John and James and the early Church. Counselling men and women who are 'islands', whether by choice persisted in or through a social isolation that cannot be overcome, is an unnatural proceeding that does not even deserve to succeed. The individual and the group must grow together.

CHAPTER 8

The Place of the Prayer Group in Healing

The New Road to Healing in the Church

There has been an already great, and could be a much greater, expansion of opportunities for healing within the Church. As against fifty years ago, the healing ministry has now been firmly established. More churches hold regular services, focused in faith on God's purpose to heal, through the presence in his Church of the living Christ. 'The same yesterday, today and forever', he heals 'all manner of sickness and disease among the people' (Heb. 13:8, Matt 4:23.) Adding depth and penetration to that expectation are the renewed gifts of the Holy Spirit, especially those of wisdom, discernment, knowledge and prophecy. When these are brought together, the deepest of hurt memories, upon which most of our neuroses, psychoses, personality disorders and chronic character defects are based, can also be healed by the Holy Spirit's operating in depth. This advance has been especially enhanced in the area of healing which covers my own speciality, that of the emotions and memories.

We are bound to be disappointed, however, by the uneven quality of service offered by the Churches and their healing prayer groups. The leaders of healing groups have no comparable training to the leaders say, of Bible study groups. We do not lay hands suddenly on enthusiastic young men and put them in charge of parishes. We train them. Training does not supplant the gifts of the Spirit. It serves to orientate the trained person to a specific ministry in the context of the human organization. This the Church always is, however much it claims also to be a vehicle for the Holy Spirit's intervention.

There need not be any dichotomy between the Churches' healing prayer groups, with their often lay leadership, and the medical and psychiatric professions. Although great strides have been made by psycho-pharmacology in the more efficient blocking of the neuro-physiological pathways by which anxiety, depression, and mind-splitting early injuries become manifest as the symptons of 'mental illness', none of us would wish to claim that these drugs *cure* mental illness. They are not, like the antibiotics, able to slay the pathogenic invaders. They are not able to be withdrawn as soon as a sharp battle is over. The maintenance of the alleviation from emotional distress depends on drug coverage for many weeks, months or years, often until external pressures have been lightened. Psychiatrists are in principle still open to the use and exploration of other alleviating and blocking agents, not to mention the possibility of some healing process which might actually eradicate and cure intractable emotional disorders.

Unwarranted Exclusions

This being so we need to be on guard against those who wish to erect barriers against healing groups, on account of their occasional shortcomings. One such critic is Professor Heribert Mühlen, in his influential book, *A Charismatic Theology*.[1] All the sufferers from the most demanding category of emotional disorder, namely 'the hysterical', and from the commonest category of emotional disturbance, 'the depressive', should in his view be diverted away from the Churches' healing prayer groups into the care, not of medical psychiatrists, but of paramedical psychologists and psychotherapists. He does not suggest that this applies only to Germany where he was writing.

There are certain passages in his book which raise grave issues of principle and practice concerning the charismatic prayer group's response to emotionally disturbed people. These questions are already the focus of difficulties and differences in Renewal prayer groups. Leaders and group members have experienced distress at not knowing how to respond to the presence in the group of people

[1] Dr H. Mühlen, *A Charismatic Theology*. Burns and Oates 1978.

suffering from what Professor Mühlen defines as 'mental illnesses', referring in particular to the diagnostic types, 'the depressive' and 'the hysteric'.

I want to clarify what, in common with some other doctors involved in the Renewal Movement, I find disturbing about the two sections where he deals with 'mental illness'. These passages establish the viewpoint I call in question (my italics).

> What is quite fundamental is that the charismatic renewal places a tremendous demand on every individual involved in it, since conversion and self-abandonment are often connected with long inward struggles and *demand mental health as a pre-condition*. Hence as a rule *prayer groups should not presume to accept as members people who are mentally ill* unless they have available an experienced psychologist or psychotherapist.[2] Those who have not been able to achieve a certain equilibrium or who *suffer from serious psychological disorders should be asked affectionately to begin by recognising the situation they are in and to look for psychotherapy* or should be directed to other possible means of coming to terms with themselves.[3]

My concern is with the renewal of charismatic prayer groups themselves. It could be objected that Professor Mühlen is concerned with specific groups of people who have gathered to study and share. It may well be that only those who have the mental energy, the concentration and the personal stamina to study theological propositions presented in these seminars can stay the course. Those who are preoccupied with their emotional pain or are overburdened by anxiety or heaviness of spirit may not be able to keep up with the week-by-week flow of teaching. If the class and the teacher press on regardless, these people could be left behind. If the leader holds up the programme to listen to them at length, the course work will not be completed on time. This can be a real difficulty. In offering seminars on pastoral care and counselling for the past twenty years, aiming to keep to a syllabus, we regularly met this conflict of priorities. But Professor Mühlen extends his observations to charismatic prayer groups in general.

In my view, church groups cannot be other than propositional filling-stations or spiritual hot-houses unless they are grounded in a realistic recognition that their members and their leaders are not

[2] Ibid., pp. 333–4.
[3] Ibid., p. 217.

only sinful people but to some degree sick people. They all have their infirmities, their ailments, their diseased and ill-functioning parts. Their minds and hearts, spirits and bodies, their feelings and their wills are also, by basic Christian definition, 'fallen'. To share in the human condition is to participate in a fallen humanity. Anxiety and depression are very common effects of that fallenness.

The so-called 'neurotic personality' is one whose primal weakness and pain press through the defences into adult consciousness. Hidden in 'the healthy' is the same sort of distress which refuses to be hidden in the person suffering from 'a nervous breakdown'. That is why the healthy are so much disturbed by the emergence of this weakness. The difference between 'the weak' and 'the strong' is, in a positive sense, one of ego-strength. The strong have received, and therefore can pass on, much that is good. But the difference is also one of inadequate or adequate defensive reaction patterns of character. Depressed people, for instance, have tried to establish repressive defences against despair. In actual depression, for various reasons, the façade of the well-defended character cracks.

Within six months or, at most, two years after the enthusiastic beginnings of any prayer group in which people are genuinely growing, it becomes apparent that all is not as it seemed at first. Some of those who started among 'the strong', with no problems, begin to demonstrate internal personality fractures quite as severe as those which were manifest in less well-defended people when the group's work began. Whether the persistence of these early injuries to trust are manifest from the beginning, or manifest themselves in the course of the group life, the purgative power of the Holy Spirit's action can work on them. Much of this suffering was laid down at the roots of the personality by the sinfulness and suffering of preceding generations. It is this bondage that the Holy Spirit seems particularly concerned to break in his work of renewal. Certainly no fundamental character change is possible unless insecure foundations are shaken, exposed and relaid. To alienate this important function, whether you call it 'emotional re-education' or 're-evaluation of basic experience' or 'therapeutic re-integration', from the life of the prayer group would be a grave loss to a work of the Spirit that is already being competently and efficiently done.

Disabling Professions

In sharp contrast, Professor Mühlen accepts the assumptions of what Ivan Illich calls 'the disabling professions'. Illich writes: 'Professions assert secret knowledge about human nature, knowledge which only they have the right to dispense. . . . They claim a monopoly over the definition of deviance and the remedies needed.'[4] As a self-accrediting élite they seek investiture by the State to prevent any 'unauthorized' persons from acting as a jury to examine eye-witnesses of their actual effectiveness. What we as medical scientists know to be hypotheses, as likely to be displaced within a decade as fashions, are put forward as facts. Dr Mühlen is in danger of betraying the Holy Spirit's capacity to fit his pastors for the task of pastoring with the gifts of wisdom, of knowledge of the heart's secrets, and of inner healing. He insists that 'illnesses' such as depression and personality disorders should be hived off from pastoral care and entrusted to 'the experts'.

Psychiatry, psychology and psychotherapy should not be gratuitously awarded an autonomy and an authority in prescribing and controlling what shall be done or not done for souls in travail. This is a competence we in these professions do not possess. Some professionals do wish to define those people whose needs or contingencies ought to be met by them alone. In the fields of psychiatry, psychotherapy and counselling, this is felt by some to be an essential restriction and the patient's only protection against malpractice. The implication of this attempted take-over from pastoral care professions, who for centuries have had a profound interest in the human personality in its sickness and its regaining health, is that they feel themselves to be 'warned off'. To take professional pastoral responsibility, for depressed, anxious, fearful, over-driven or despairing personalities is now felt by many priests and pastors to be about as heinous a trespass as taking services in another man's parish without his permission.

I am by no means alone among psychiatrists in discerning an even greater danger from this professional expansionism and possessiveness. It is that ordinary people feel, and are made and meant to feel, distrustful of their God-given intuitive faculties, shamefaced about their natural competence, and thus over-ready to back off from helping others, pleading a disqualifying ignorance.

[4] I. Illich, *Disabling Professions*, Marion Boyars 1977.

This is no sort of response to the logistics of health care in these days. The residential care of disturbed people, especially of the young and the old, cannot keep up, on the one hand with rising costs, and on the other with the steadily rising incidence of those who now live on into adult life to suffer these disorders. The economics of the Health Service and the Social Services are such that no appreciable expansion of the numbers of mental health professionals can be looked for. The future does not lie there, except to a limited and almost insignificant extent. Social workers are becoming severely overburdened in their attempts to care for emotionally disturbed individuals, families and communities, as well as baffled by the expectations placed on them by people who have become, especially in urban areas, increasingly passive. These global expectations are intrinsically unreasonable, unnatural and, one must even say, crushing and inhuman.

In rural communities, it is still possible to discern the natural pattern of reciprocal help, given and received, at times of crisis and stress. All who live within the parish boundaries are accepted as part of the Church's and the community's responsibility. This essential mutual help operates first within families, as a form of brotherly and sisterly self-help. Neighbourhoods can be structured as an extension of that natural self-help when a family cannot cope. It comes into being on a district or even national level when a neighbourhood's power of self-help is overwhelmed by larger disasters. Experts can and do come to the aid of these natural structures of mutual help at each level, but only where their expertise is appropriate, never as a substitute for basic caring.

My own experience as a mental health professional is shared by many others. It gives me real satisfaction when an individual or family is referred to me by a caring group or community. I am able to exercise my proper skills, either by enlarging for them the possibilities for further progress, or by helping them to accept, without guilt or restlessness, what in the nature of things cannot be changed.

What is deeply burdensome and provokes in me what I feel to be a justifiable sorrow and anger, is to have someone referred to me, not for a consultation about how to increase the effectiveness of Christian befriending, but to be henceforth the only person now willing to befriend this difficult person. The Christian caring group has been pushed up against an intensity or complexity of mental and emotional pain which they have found to be alarming, and in the end, unbearable. The mental pain and emotional disturbance in 'the patient' has reverberated into areas of past experience in their own lives which have been more or less successfully repressed. They are only too willing to believe that they should not have presumed to accept such a person in their prayer group or intimate church fellowship in the first place.

In deeply troubled people, the overlap between the psychological material and the affairs of the human spirit is too extensive to justify this type of distinction. What makes it particularly troublesome to the Christian pastor whose concern is with the human spirit, is that the very existence of *man as spirit* is a concept which many mental health professionals as behavioural scientists would reject, if they could make sense of it at all. This blindness to life in the Spirit is too momentous for practitioners of pastoral care to hand over their troubled people to the secular professionals' care and control. It would be wise to ask their advice, certainly, in matters where they possess expertise. But that is a very different thing from handing over troubled individuals, expecting the secular arm to exercise authority, guidance, control and pressure within a régime or insti-tution which claims total authority over the person, until the symp-toms have abated and the ability to function 'normally' has been, in their opinion, restored.

The more active the psychological intervention undertaken, the greater the risk of manipulation away from faith; not just away from a pseudo-faith, which anyone might welcome, but from all faith in God, as being a kind of contemptible refuge for inadequate person-alities. I was caring once for a woman who had been sent by Christian people to attend regular group therapy in a day hospital, with the assurance that 'Christ meant her to co-operate with this therapy fully'. In fact the group was conducted in ways which would bring it under sharp criticism from most experienced group leaders. Violent expressions of anger against parents were the pass-port to entry into the inner circle of the group. This atmosphere of encouraged and indulged hatred proved very devastating for the woman. The whole procedure was the more baffling because when she protested to her Christian friends that this was harming her, they denied the possibility.

There are, of course, aspects of mental illness so severe and so bizarre, that attendance at a prayer group is unlikely to be useful and the need for institutional psychiatric care is paramount and obvious. The law gives rights of certification to certain registered psychiatrists to commit to institutional care sufferers from psychotic illness who are likely to harm themselves or others. This legislation is safeguarded to a limited extent by requiring the consent of a social worker if the family cannot or will not give theirs.

The Hysterical Personality in the Prayer Group

Hysterical persons can be troublesome in prayer groups and I understand the longing to steer them into psychotherapy. Hysterical personality disorders are, as Dr Main of the Cassel Hospital showed,[5] an 'ailment' so disruptive of the smooth running of a hospital ward that early discharge of the troublemaker is the sovereign psychiatric remedy. It has been said that the difference between a skilled and experienced psychiatrist and a beginner is that the senior man recognizes the hysteric quicker and runs away faster!

This is no place to expand on the care of those who suffer from this dreadful compulsive need to attract and hold human attention. They have a skill in manipulating self-conscious helpers who try too hard, while 'put up' for certain failure, which is quite devastating. Those who are unaware of their own compulsive need to be helpful to others are recognized by the hysterical person to be what they are, not actual helpers, but people in need of someone to 'help'. Almost from the beginning of the interchange, the hysterical patient is in control of the helping situation, not the so-called helper. True helpers of hysterical personalities are tough enough and fair enough to gain and keep ultimate control of the situation. A truly loving insight into what is going on, into the devious ways in which one is being seduced and the subtle ways in which one's unavowed needs are being met, is a pre-requisite if we are to establish a relationship which the hysterical person will respect. If they know more about us than we are prepared to know about ourselves, they are the experts, we are being bamboozled. While flattering the all-too-willing victim, she (or he) will secretly be despising the fantasy-laden helper, preparing to pounce when they have caught him or her out. The beseeching child in them becomes, in a flash, a terrifying parent-like critic, scorning the incompetence of what

[5] T. Main 'The Ailment', *Journal of Medical Psychology*, (1957), XXX, Part 3 pp. 129ff.

they choose to see as betrayal. Picking on some technical infringe-
ment of the helping relationship, or failure to back up some totally
impracticable promise of total support, carefully extracted in some
unguarded moment, the weak and needy 'hysteric' suddenly becomes a tyrannical judge. The person enjoys the reversal of roles
and the opportunity to despise and humiliate the gullible helper,
who so recently was basking in the warmth of an unprecedented
appreciation. He or she feels a wicked satisfaction in exposing the
basic dishonesty of those who live by their *fantasies* of being 'helpers',
never admitting that they, too, need help.

These situations do not often happen in prayer groups. The
leader, unless he or she has foolishly consented to a private agenda
to give extra-special help to this extra-specially needy one, has the
support of the men and women in the group to give the necessary
feedback and exercise firm control. The leader is able to protect her
– or him – from scapegoating and rejection by dismissive elements
in the group. The pastoral task is to deprive her of the satisfaction
of the outright rejection that she expects and engineers, while firmly
holding up the mirror of truth to those objectionable or self-dra-
matizing aspects of her behaviour which sometimes, whether consciously or unconsciously, are calculated to make others despair of
her. The group models itself on the style of the leadership, siding
with the hysterical person's adult self to gain control over this
demanding child inside her. Unless prevented, the demanding child
persistently takes control, dominating the situation until it turns to
her own destruction. The support of a mature group is the very
relationship she most needs as a means to growth.

The toughness and tenderness of Christ's dealings with the three
recorded women in his life whom others expected him to recognize
and reject, is the model for his disciples now. The average psychiatrist, the doctors and mental nursing officers of our day are
probably no more tolerant in their dealings with these infuriatingly
difficult women than were the average Pharisees, the doctors of the
law, and religious leaders in New Testament times.

The Holy Spirit is well able to give to ordinary men and women,
ministering together, an accurate and empathetic discernment of
the disguised disparities between word and act that the hysterical
person relies upon to dominate others, while seeming to be asking
for help. Ordinary Christians as human beings have this capacity,
unless some self-styled expert robs them of their sense of com-

petence. Professional posturing here is an illusion, and I would wish to promote sober confidence in the biblical theology of pastoral care. Pastoral care-givers can trust in the Holy Spirit's quite adequate gifts for ministry. They can rely on their enlightened common sense in observing what is going on in hysterically manipulated relationships. Our principal danger is to give in to the fantasy that we can minister to such persons on our own. If they demand this private attention, this must be seen as the first move in the power game to control the over-eager helper. Toughness is more truly loving here than indulgent tenderness.

The leader's problem, if he or she cannot control the person who unreasonably demands group time and attention, is his weakness, not his meekness. He or she needs to spot the difference between the genuine intention to contribute or inquire, and the latent (to them) but patent (to others) situation when they are losing the sympathy of the group and building up hostility. Maintaining unity while encouraging sharing in determining the agenda of a group is an essential leadership skill which, by its very nature, has to deal empathetically and firmly with disruptions that come from private agendas. Training may well be needed for this leadership function. But let us not fall into the theological error of divorcing such skills from the pastoral office, and, slavish to the spirit of the age, handing them over to secular 'experts'. The right experts could assist in the training of the leadership in these skills, but they must not be allowed to displace them from ministry of the Church.

New Testament doctrine is clear enough. It does not envisage pastoral care empowered by the Holy Spirit as being incomplete and ineffective until the epiphany of some latter-day sophists of the psyche who will take over all the difficult cases. The task of theology, as David Wells suggests, is:

in part to explore and analyse the modern mind and develop ways of linking it to the biblical doctrine of Christ's conquest over the devil in whose chilling grasp the whole world is held. . . . Christ delivers people from this tyranny by 'disarming' the powers of darkness, revealing the nature of their deception of people, releasing from the hands of sin those who trust him, reversing the inward disintegration of their nature, breaking open their prison house brought on through death, and cancelling their penalty.[6]

It is for this reason that 'theology is always and inescapably a work of "enculturation" . . . Doctrine abhors novelty, theology in both its defensive and interpretive roles, requires it.'[7] Charismatic theology is well based in New Testament doctrine. When it grapples with the spirit of the age, it finds, in our age, an obeisance to the experts – in this case the mental illness professionals – which it must either interpret as God's gift to the Church, or limit and qualify, defending pastoral care against a doctrinally unwarranted take-over. Where the overlap between the sacred and the secular subject-matter is as extensive as it is between total pastoral care of deeply troubled people as envisaged by New Testament doctrine, and their total re-allocation to psychiatric care, theology alone has the task of making the necessary discriminations from a Christian point of view.

The Mentally Ill

When defensiveness without insight is replaced by the inescapable onset of breakdown there is no doubt about the reality of the mental pain. The problem is that while it is 're-membered' as such, it is neither accurately identified as of early origin, nor connected up to the incidents which initially provoked it. Dr Mühlen writes: 'In that case it is only an experienced psychotherapist who can help them towards becoming aware of their illness.' But, if a breakdown has occurred, so that an unsupported adult is floundering in the mess in which their inner child of the past still lives, they are already aware enough of their illness. What they are not aware of is the assimilative strength which their adult self is capable of, in Christ, by the power of the Holy Spirit. The intimate prayer group, gathered for counselling, applies to them, in specific detail, faith in a living Lord. This faith has been liberated in the worship, in the ministry of the Word and in the corporate and individual responses in relation to it.

In fact, the transition from insightless and defensive living to an insightful recognition of need comes about best precisely within the

[6] D. F. Wells, *The Search for Salvation*. (Inter Varsity Press, 1978), p. 41.
[7] Ibid p. 42.

atmosphere of a faith that justifies, accepts and welcomes us in our weaknesses as well as in our strengths. In such supportive, prayerful and sharing groups, the secrets of a man's heart are opened up to him by their united witness to the truth, about what God is really like and what man's inner being is really like. This leads, not to a breakdown or failure of existing neurotic defences, but to a break-through in which the strengthened and supported adult becomes aware of hitherto hidden weaknesses and hurts and brings them boldly into consciousness. In sharing them with the prayer coun-sellors he brings Christ into them, so as to bear them and to share them with him. This integrative process leads to a re-evaluation of their meaning in adult terms. The unloved child no longer feels guilty about being unloved. The parentless child accepts the original shame. In spite of infantile experience reverberating from the past, the adult relies in the Spirit upon the assurance of a new heredity, new family membership as a child of God. I am supported in this interpretation of what happens, in ordinarily competent charismatic prayer counselling, by many authors (e.g. Scanlan, McNutt, East and others[8]) and particularly by the chapter on 'Healing' in John Gunstone's *A People for his Praise*.[9]

If prayer groups, in a dilettante fashion advertised their services as 'free-psychotherapy' they would be acting in misleading com-petition with psychotherapists. Psychotherapy is practised by ex-pensively trained professionals who charge or are salaried for their services, providing a named, recognized and identifiable approach to the cure of emotional illness or the re-education of badly learned infantile experiences of life. There is no risk of offending ethically unless we offer a named brand of therapy which we are not com-petent to practise.

Christ is still, through his Church, calling to himself those who are overburdened and in total weariness. He calls the fearful and those in bondages of every kind, the anxious and the broken, so that in experiencing, through his Body, the intimate caring of the Father and the sharing of suffering by the Saviour they can be at peace again. But neither Christ nor the Christian body is offering psycho-analysis or psychotherapy as an identifiable professional skill. Knot-

[8] M. Scanlan, *Inner Healing*. New York, Paulist Press. F. McNutt, *Healing*. Notre Dame, Indiana, Ave Maria Press. R. East, *Heal the Sick*. Hodder and Stoughton 1977.
[9] J. A. Gunstone, *People for His Praise*. Hodder and Stoughton 1978.

ted minds may indeed be analysed, that is, loosened, and distorted emotions may be healed, but the agent is the redemptive love of God in Christ through the Church's ministry. It is not a secular discipline.

In Britain professional psychotherapeutic help is not easily come by, even for the middle-class person. Outside London very little such help is available. We have, in Britain, steadily discouraged psychologists from entering the profession of psychotherapy. Their field has been personality and intelligence testing. At best it is often an offer of behavioural conditioning in a characteristically (though not necessarily) Godless milieu. Most psychotherapists would reject outright the task of preparing the mentally ill so as to be readmitted, when the worst is over, to a prayer group. Since most talking therapies do not go very deep and have little concept of primal injuries, their aim is, as Freud's was, unashamedly to assist the patient to put into operation somewhat less disabling defences. The basic anguish of being human is covered up more skilfully and with less disturbance to relationships.

In the United States, pastoral counsellors are not hard to come by, but it is a sad fact that there is, I understand, no group of ministers of religion there who have given such a cool reception as the pastoral counsellors have to the charismatic ministry. That may change. I hope that it will and I work for that as I have opportunity. Christ's invitation to burdened people is to come to him to be relieved by his bearing and sharing of the pain, replacing the injurious yoke by one that is 'easy' and a burden that is 'light'. If Christians are in any sense representative of Christ, those who are burdened should come boldly into our midst with the expectation that they will find relief.

The prayer group leader must learn to recognize and name the condition called 'depression' which oppresses or possesses a brother, so as to deliver him from it into a full, victorious membership of the prayer group. The sort of depressed people who are unsuitable for groups are those who misunderstand the teaching about 'looking into their own souls' and overdo it. The depressed people who are in error admitted to a group are unable to relate at all, being too heavily pressured by guilt feelings. What is a manageable level of guilt feeling in average group members has become excessive in the over-depressed individual. There is also a need to discriminate, which basic pastoral instruction must teach, between recognizably neurotic, chronic, persistent guilt feelings on the one hand, and that genuine conviction of sin which leads to repentance on the other. The one, the neurotic guilt, is removed by Christ's 'slaying of the Law'. When it is applied at the appropriate depth, it is effective in shifting the grounds of our acceptance of our own identity from works to faith. On the other hand, genuine conviction of sin leads at once to repentance and is met at once by the Father's forgiveness in Christ. It needs no time-consuming penitential grovelling or chronic guilt feelings to prove its genuineness on our part. Authentic conviction of sin leads, sooner rather than later, to praise and freedom of conscience. We must discern the difference between chronic guilt feelings, the crushing burden of perpetual self-accusation, and that necessary conviction of sin which leads us to repentance as soon as our heart and will consent and convert to its verdict. Failure in discernment may lead us to send the bewildered depressed person away like an untouchable to the psychiatrist.

Dr Mühlen, whom I criticized earlier, writes, about praying for discernment, these words of wisdom:

> We must all be prepared to learn from history and to pray to God urgently for the gift of discernment. This gift too is granted only to someone who is receptive towards it, who surrenders himself completely to God and does not act merely according to the rules of human prudence. Anyone who prays for the gift of discernment assumes at the same time that there really is something to discern, that the impulses of the Holy Spirit are not the same as our own impulses. This distinction is all the more important in that the tendency to sin and thus also to the misuse of the gifts of the Spirit is ineradicable.[10]

The group leader will pray for this gift of discernment, so as to be able to know when and where the healing power of Christ is to be actualized in the deep places of the depressed mind, heart and spirit. New Testament doctrine nowhere suggests that there is a category of 'depressed' person to whom the Gospel does not apply, and who lies at the uttermost range of the Holy Spirit's competence. The task of charismatic pastoral theology is to grapple with the 'enculturing' of that doctrine, demonstrating its continuance under the special circumstances of our time.

[10] Dr H. Mühlen, op. cit., p. 173.

CHAPTER 9

Understanding and Counselling the Violent

I intend here to explore the correlation between a particular piece of research into the psychodynamic and psychopathological origins of violence and the symbolic theology that goes out to meet it from the crucifixion of Jesus. This sort of correlation has been explored already by several authors and pastoral counsellors, at the depth then available, in relation to the neuroses and personality disorders of the European and American conforming middle classes. What of those 'delinquent' members who do not adapt to this same cultural system but are at violent odds with it, especially in adolescence and early adult life. The problem is mostly among boys, but is manifested with great ferocity among some adolescent girls.

I have been pressed to this inquiry by the recognition, by prison chaplains and probation officers who have attended our five-day residential groups to work on themselves, that our new paradigm, the maternal-foetal distress syndrome, is 'ringing all sorts of bells' in relation to their imprisoned clients or unruly probationers. Before we or others attempt any organizational response to requests that may be in the offing, for Christian, or more general pastoral counselling intervention, in a field where the therapeutic approach has so often come unstuck, let us see what resources and guidelines we might have to offer.

Hans Selye's work on stress, known as the General Adaptation Syndrome, was becoming known when I was a medical student in the early thirties. Yet the first number of the first volume of *The Official Journal of the International Institute of Stress and its Affiliates*, entitled 'Stress' only appeared in spring 1980. The first article, by the Nobel Prize Winner for Medicine in 1953, Professor Sir Hans

Krebs, is somewhat surprisingly on 'Biological Aspects of Juvenile Delinquency'.

He notes that a marked deterioration in adolescent behaviour has been taking place over a period when people have been materially much better off than ever before. Material deprivation is therefore not the cause. He shows that the enormous increase in delinquency during recent decades almost exclusively involves young people. The London police statistics reveal that over 50% of all delinquents caught by the police in London are twenty-one and below. Many kinds of crime, such as vandalism and mugging, were virtually non-existent in Britain twenty-five years ago, so eliminating genetic causes. 'We are left with environmental factors and we have to identify those which have changed and have had an influence on young people.' The most important, but insufficiently acknowledged, influences seem to him to lie in three great changes which have taken place during the last two decades.

Three Great Changes

The three great changes Hans Krebs believes to be significant are in 1) parent-child relationships, 2) pupil-teacher relationships, and 3) the judiciary.

He summarizes the changes in relationships that have taken place in these three areas as 'pampering and spoiling'.

> Parents spoil and pamper the child instead of providing an environment in which it will learn to cope with life, will be keen to try new experiences and will respect the limits imposed by society. The educational system pampers and spoils the pupil instead of providing an environment in which he or she will learn to concentrate on and enjoy his studies, respect authority, and adapt himself to changing circumstances. Society spoils and pampers its citizens by luring them from self-reliance and independence by providing high and easy-to-come-by social security benefits. Instead it should provide work and the opportunity for further education in skills, knowledge and citizenship.

No doubt correctly, he sees a common factor here in that all three environments are no longer insisting on limits, no longer requiring a certain level of responsible behaviour to be shown, and are failing to provide firm resistance to socially irresponsible behaviour. Had these been provided by 'authority' they could have been internalized in the young adults as their own standards and reaffirmed by experience that they work well. Neglecting them as we have done plunges all the participants into a painful chaos. Krebs summarizes this virtual delinquency in parents, teachers and magistrates/judges as 'pampering and spoiling'.

But the social symptoms of behavioural disorder in the delinquent young are not the kind regularly and predictably associated with 'pampering and spoiling'. That leads to the self-indulgent, coddled personality that expects to be waited on hand and foot without contributing any personal effort to the enterprise to make it healthily mutual.

What is complained of in the behaviour of adolescent youth is 'violence, vandalism, hooliganism', wanton destruction of trees, lamp-posts, sign-posts, and amenity seats; slashing the tyres of parked cars; smashing window-panes and breaking into houses', there to slash couches and chairs or to foul carpets with excreta, which is a specific kind of 'pointless' violence. There are also violent muggings, in which some retributive satisfaction is evidently gained by kicking the victim in the stomach, the teeth, or the face, blacking his or her eyes.

It in no way accords with my experience of psychodynamic origins to attribute this intense and symbolically loaded violence to the laissez-faire *pampering by parents, teachers or judges.* At best they could only restrain such violence more effectively.

Spoiling, with over-indulgence, does produce ill-effects in the young. They need to test their boundaries by pushing hard on parents. They will push even harder on pampering parent-figures, forcing them to react, cry halt, and so allow the child to discover the limits of the family's, the school's or society's tolerance. But that is far from this kind of paroxysmal mayhem* with all its indications of reprisal, of paying back old scores with a vengeance and in kind. If parents have been too soft they may well become an easy push-over, but that is no adequate cause for such insensate outbursts of violent attack.

Let us look more closely at the sociological change which Hans Krebs regards as most important. He finds it in *the sudden rise in the incidence of married women going out to work.* They must leave their infants under five years old and often much earlier, to be looked after by someone else. He refers to the work of John Bowlby, Rene

Spitz, Simon Yudkin, Hugh Jolly, Mia Pringle and the Hassen-
steins, all of whom showed the importance of close relationships
between the mother and her baby, from birth and breast-feeding
on. He writes:

> An ever-increasing number of mothers have taken up full-time
> employment. In Britain the number of fully employed women
> has tripled since 1950. They want to earn money and perhaps
> get away from the loneliness and drudgery of housework. This
> changes   the   focus   of   their   interests,   and   their
> regular absences. . .diminish the close relationship.

This is true, but the main consequences, in manifest behaviour, of
such maternal absences and failure of bonding are the hysterical
personality disorders, or agoraphobic reactions or both. If that
absence goes on too long, the baby will give up hope and switch
into trans-marginal distress. This, then, typically leads to a withdrawn, schizoid personality reaction. Violent clinging or pushing
away are common in those who have been thus deprived, but not
destroying by uprooting, slashing, kicking and fouling.

   If all attempts to manipulate or persuade people to fall in line
with the hystero-schizoid demand (to have them come closer, or,
according to mood, stay further away) fail, then another kind of
withdrawal takes place. They take back their investment in a real,
if hard-to-manage, struggle to control the 'distance' of others, how
near or far away they are supposed to stay. They lapse into the
low-grade defences of denial of present reality and projection of an
old one. They block out stubborn reality and cling more stubbornly
to the misperceptions and misinterpretation of a paranoid reaction.
This has its own violent feelings, but it is into a litigious frenzy that
it leads, not into a bloodbath of violence or an orgy of smashing,
tearing up or tearing out things or defiling them.

The Maternal-Foetal Distress Syndrome

If the findings of recent research into psycho-pathological origins
hold up under repeated test, we can with some confidence attribute
this youthful destructiveness to the fixation of an invasive violence
which penetrated the foetus in the womb. It is a retaliatory response
to the malignant influx, through the umbilical circulation, of the

vehement passions of a distressed mother, herself responding to the overt or hidden violence of her own social context.

There is a rustle of protest when a mother returns to work too soon after the birth of her baby, but there has so far been no hint that it makes any difference at all to the foetus, what she does with herself or others do to her, in the three months following conception. Typically she carries on working, packing in more activity, bearing in mind the months of limitation which birth and the total demand of the new-born baby will bring. Were she to remain at home, concentrating on being a mother to the children already part of the family, or attending with tranquillity and lively expectancy of spirit, mind and body to her new assignment of motherhood, she could provide the milieu of tenderness and delight in creating, in which the fast-growing foetus could thrive.

Of course, being at home by no means ensures this exemplary environment for the foetus. Every kind of social distress, at whatever level, in the family, the neighbourhood, the local community, and on to the national and global systems, impinges on the woman. The message of these surroundings penetrates into her spirit and whole person, an influx of emotion and contextual sense which she shares with the foetus embedded in her.

Every item of distress operating against full humanness and caring within the community inevitably feeds through into the pregnant woman. This happens first at the intimate level of her marriage. Active brutality on the part of the husband may be uncommon, but she may suffer from a perhaps crueller neglect, should he ignore the naturally stronger needs of the newly-pregnant woman for more assured protection and closer-drawing intimacy. These subtler forms of 'violent' deprivation are woefully common. Men of all classes can be at their worst when this, to them mysterious, process begins. Being pregnant is one function they can never be better at than their womenfolk. Some show their resentment at their now disputed possession of the woman's body by withdrawal of affection. Others sulk like small boys, fomenting stormy incidents to give mean expression to their sense of hurt.

This can be a time, too, when the resolution of all wise partners in marriage to *leave* the father and mother, in order to *cleave* to each other, can be painfully tested. If the husband stands closer to his wife, to share the added strain, the pregnancy experience becomes what Hans Selye called 'eustress', good stress, growth-promoting stress, the opposite of distress. But if the husband harbours a basic splitness engendered in his own relationship with his own mother, the now maternal status of the maiden he had married may scare him. He reminds himself of other more urgent 'duties' that demand his full attention, to which, with unconscious gratitude, he turns. The unsuccoured wife is bound to undergo immense turmoil, bitter disappointment and perhaps outbursts or, more likely, 'inbursts' of justifiable anger. She may regress, actually or emotionally, running back home, rejecting the husband and the marriage. These violent emotions, whether yearnings or revulsions, as all our present researches show, pass, in some as yet unfathomed way, into the placental circulation, entering the foetus through the umbilical cord.

To be kept, in spite of surrounding anxiety, in peace of heart, is possible for the mother whose mind is stayed on God's unfailing fathering, but hardly otherwise. The Virgin Mother of Jesus, whose husband at this time of shocked discovery of her pregnant state was minded to put her away privily to mitigate the terrible disgrace, had this to cope with and a foetus within her to protect. That Jesus was kept without splitting here, with its entail of sin, we owe to the total faithfulness and undeflected assent of the Blessed Virgin to the road of her Son's Cross, as his Father asked it of her.

The re-emergence of maternal-foetal distress occurs in the course of pre-natal integration work when a man or woman who is undertaking the reliving of life in the womb during the first three months (or first 'trimester') after conception, comes to the point where a helper places three fingers over the navel to represent and simulate the establishment of the umbilical circulation. This 'tree of life', with its roots spreading out into the placenta, its trunk the short stout cord, and its branches the veins and arteries spreading out from the navel into the foetal body, should be for the transmission, not only of the good nutrients for the fast-growing body, but also of the mother's sustained and sustaining spirit. The foetus, we find, responds both generally and specifically to what goes on in the mother's world. Whatever matters most to her gets through to the foetus, of course with a most primitive kind of comprehension.

John the Baptist, you will remember, 'leapt in the womb' of his mother, Elizabeth, as she met her cousin Mary with the Christ-child in her. This stray text in the scriptures does not establish the fact of maternal-foetal emotional transfer or of shared 'umbilical affect' during pre-natal life. It just hints at the connection. When what is thrusting its way into the foetus is not good but is made up of bursts of anger, paroxysms of bitterness, grief or despair, fits of fury, these emotions are packing impulses of violence into the mother's own clenched jaws, fists and feet, tensing her muscles with adrenergic preparations for fight or flight. Judging by the violence of the adult response at this juncture the foetus certainly experiences precisely the same emotions, and at what seems to be an equivalent intensity. But the foetus has no means of comprehending what the furore is about. It knows only that it is forced to submit to a penetrating thrust of violent and painful feeling, most commonly represented as a transfixing spear or great (often 'rusty') nail of affliction, thrust in at the navel. It is by no means clear *why* this should be so or what mechanism is involved. *That* it is so, and is relived as such, we can no longer doubt.

Violent Reactions

The impulse to rip out the cord is immensely strong, as strong as the foetal limbs are weak. The person working at integrating prenatal experience is encouraged to give an adult voice (which was not, of course, able to function in the womb) to the foetus, now to moan, roar or scream out the pain that has been muted since it first occurred. We have no stereotype of a 'primal scream'. The deep inspiration, 'up into the adult', 'here and now', is followed by a long expiration, with a neutral sound, as attention focuses down into the reception of the foetal experience, 'there and then'. The neutral sound changes as it gathers the force and specificity of the foetal affect with which contact is being made. It frequently changes, from fear to anger, from contentment to tearfulness and on into terror. In a similar way, the foetus finds its own adult hands, feeling 'terribly small' and as feeble in effect as they are powerful in intention, trying to tear away the hand of the facilitator that represents the cord attached at the navel.

An article in the *British Medical Journal* (26 January 1980, p. 234) says: 'Nine weeks after conception the baby is well enough formed for him to bend his fingers round an object in the palm of his hand. At twelve weeks he can close the finger and thumb.' So what our subjects do, feeling that they are repeating what they tried to do as foetus, by way of tugging at the cord, somehow sensed as the entry point for the distress, is quite feasible, given this primitive symbolism.

On other occasions they counter-attack with one or both feet. As Mott wrote and our subjects confirm they represent both the attacked placenta and the attacking foetus. The two umbilical arteries spring from the two iliac arteries that flow into the legs. Hence the legs represent those two umbilical arteries which, so close by, symbolically return affect to the mother, along with substances to be excreted. So they kick, with intent to destroy, violently against the placental source of the 'black and bitter bile' that enters at the navel and spreads its 'vileness' everywhere. It is a retributive cruelty that they intend. Those who can respond with aggressive violence are determined to inflict hurt, tit-for-tat, exactly paying back what was inflicted upon them at a time of unsuspecting innocence and vulnerability. That is why, according to this interpretation, the targets for the mugger's attack are carefully chosen, not to give any satisfaction of winning in fair combat with a worthy foe possessing some parity of strength, but are selected to replicate as closely as possible the original intent to commit mayhem, with one notable change, that the original *victim* of the intra-uterine violence is no longer the victim but the assailant. He has switched, to fulfil the primal determination and its concomitant fantasy, to be, this time, top-dog, not under-dog.

In this symbolic scene, the 'pointless' hooliganism complained of, breaking or uprooting trees, lamp-posts and road-signs makes excellent sense. It is the bad cord they are attacking. Our less overtly delinquent subjects, on reflection, remember doing or planning to do similar things, with a fierce delight which they did not understand at all at this time, but do now. They make all such connections. I make no interpretations during 'therapy', such as I am doing here. 'Slashing the tyres of parked cars', means 'taking the wind out of' those circular structures (suggestive, perhaps, of the placenta) that belong to the privileged. Seeing them collapse and gloating over the discomfiture of the proud and felt-to-be-stingy owners, what could better this as an act of symbolic retribution – short of kicking them in the teeth.

This sort of violence amounts to a displaced counter-attack of the foetus on the bad placenta, which is distinctly felt to suck the foetal energy or life out of it, or give too little to survive on, or actually to inject foul feelings. This retaliation occurs when foetal courage takes strength from despair and does not care if it 'dies' in the attempt. At other times, the fantasy of some act of malicious trickery is all that the fear-instilled foetus can rise to, both at the time, and later when the same scene is being enacted, or acted-out, in the 'adult' world, in some hit-and-run escapade.

Where the mother (some time after the foetus senses that she knows that it is alive and present in her womb), decides to pay no attention to it, and instead to gad about in her restless round of attention-taking activities in the world 'out there', there is foetal bafflement, leading to deep resentment. She is refusing to recognize her changed status or give any priority, at any time of day or night, to sending inner messages of attentiveness or of welcome to the new arrival. It feels an unwelcome stranger. When this inaccessibility of hers is experienced, the image of the mother as living on the far side of a sheet of 'plate glass' is quite common. Certainly, 'breaking glass' is a way of 'getting through' to an insensitive, inattentive, mother, who has a foetus growing in her, but never takes the trouble to 'call it to mind'. Or, when things have gone too far to be reme- died, it is a smashing to break away to some other reality. A number of 'integrators' have recognized this 'glass smashing' as a symbolic equivalent to their intra-uterine urge to break through into the absent mother, or out of her.

'Breaking and entering', and there slashing what is private and valuable to the privileged class, and particularly depositing (back) the filthy excreta with which one has felt 'stuffed', is acting out with a vengeance and full of symbolic logic. The two umbilical arteries serve the actual function of excretion to the foetus. They are also (as Francis Mott pointed out nearly thirty years ago from his analy- sis of dreams) the symbolic route for counter-attack of the foetus on the placenta/mother. Four-letter-words have the same vigour and scatological force; 'sod off', 'fuck you', 'piss off', or 'you're just shit', are common equivalents, more expressive than polite.

The alimentary tract is the tube, pre-eminently, into which bad 'umbilical affect' is displaced. If the rich 'make me feel sick', to be sick or to spit on this property gives a sense of just requital. Since evacuation of the badness *per rectum* is a privilege only undertaken by the foetus under great terror *in utero*, to do this on someone else's patch gives some satisfaction.

Correlation?

It may be objected that my evidence, correlating violent personality disorders with the maternal-foetal distress syndrome, is not drawn from work with those who have been imprisoned for violence, or who escaped leaving a trail of destruction behind them. At this stage, obviously not. The objection is met, as far as it can be, by pointing out, as our probation officers and prison chaplain did, that the exact parallels of the forms of criminal violence were part of the fantasies and feelings expressed by 'non-delinquent' subjects in our group. In the context of their own foetal encounter with the vile influx of 'umbilical affect' they had been able, acceptably, to explore and give violent expression to the emotions of counter-destructiveness. These violent emotions had emerged from time to time, accompanied by specific feelings of loss of capacity to protect the boundaries of the self from invasion by destructive 'stuff', a syndrome with body-mind-spirit aspects they recognized as identical with what they had experienced when re-living the distress of the first trimester.

Later in life, various social restraints, loves and fears and accepted responsibilities had enabled them to achieve control, inhibiting their 'acting-out' of the violence they felt and fantasied. This power alone seems to separate the suppressed violence in the custodian from the expressed violence of the criminal. It is often remarked that the afflicted, who take the blame of the mother's distress, despair and bitter anger upon themselves, clinging to the notion that they are the evil cause of her pain, feel intensely guilty, whereas criminals, who in society's book ought to feel guilty, in fact do not. If they are, as this explanation suggests, simply operating a talion law, an eye for an eye and a tooth for a tooth, is it so surprising that they feel like officers of a more just law, a forgotten law? Their failure, at this motivational level, to feel guilty, is based on the surely correct conviction that in the womb, when the persecution began, they were certainly not guilty. How should we expect them now to feel guilty, when, as it seems to them they are simply retaliating, having found, in some present-day repetition of the old injustice, or something near enough, a trigger for the old gun.

Remedy

Hans Krebs' remedy for this violence is stronger parenting, with less pampering, less permissiveness and more firm discipline. He hopes this will come about mainly by good parent/teacher example, and by their insisting on the fulfilment of social duties and responsibilities. I agree most heartily that this swing into dilatory, laggardly, altogether-too-easy-going parenting has gone too far, in reaction to a generation of such strictness as often broke the child's spirit, disheartening and discouraging them contrary to Paul's apostolic injunction to Christian fathers. It would indeed be good for those who were so afflicted in the womb as to have been incensed with violent anger, to be brought up, after birth (hopefully a not too crushing or asphyxiating one) in a family practising outgoing love to each other and with internal self-discipline for the good and freedom of all, both family and neighbours. It might well persuade them to forgo their vengeance.

However, Christian theological realities should warn us against optimism about any radical change, by means simply of firm and kindly discipline. In cases such as these, who are the victims of serious offences against primal justice, the hurt now buried in the depths of their souls and spirits cannot easily be forgiven, the more so since repression has blotted out the original context. They have an almost crusading determination to seek revenge. God's remedy for them is not even his own fatherly care, precious though that will become. Nor does God rely on the rules he gave 'for our own good always', which in the patriarchal tradition the father told his son as he rehearsed the law's just provisions.

The command to be merciful stands in the way of personal vengeance. 'Vengeance is mine', says the Lord. What does he mean by that? The vengeance of this Lord God is nothing other than the Cross of Christ. The Passion of Christ is God's way of retaliating, by a similar *suffering*. This enactment of divine affliction is God's eternal apology to all the innocent afflicted. He stands among them, sharing their fate, but he does it willingly. He is identified in every point with them, in each pain. We read, however, that 'When *he* suffered, he threatened not,' whereas they, unable to bear it without bitterness, are still breathing out fire and slaughter. God's vengeance was, paradoxically and with staggering redemptive logic, to take the vengeance of man upon his own most vulnerable body and sensitive person.

The Crucified was no stranger to affliction. When he came to his own people, like the foetus into its own womb, so far from recognizing and receiving him, they soon planned to murder him and once to stone him. His power to deliver men from demonic powers they attributed to the Prince of Devils. He was hounded from place to place, persecuted particularly by the religious who wanted to abort both him and his ministry. His powerful goodness attracted a bitter envy that did not leave off attacking him until it had nailed his hands and feet to a dead tree and left him to die. A soldier thrust a spear into his battered body, still bleeding from the lash and the buffeting. The crushing weight of the cross-beam lay on his back and the crown of thorns was crushed on his head.

The appropriateness of this remedy, for the primeval violence that fights back from a violent womb, is staggering in its matching provisions. Yet it was planned, in the purposes of God, from the foundation of the world. The remedy pre-dates man's sickness. The Lamb was, as God's costly gift to mankind, 'slain' before the world began. It was carried through, in recorded time and in human history, by the One who was crucified for claiming he was God's Son.

There is a fury in all afflicted persons, as strong in those who never put a foot wrong by the law as in those who do. This anger insists that whoever is responsible for this appalling suffering should be made to suffer. He should taste his own bitter medicine. Within the Holy Trinity that cry for justice was heard. The Incarnation and Passion of the Second Person, the only Son of the Father, is the acceptance of that challenge from the heart of the Eternal.

The compulsively violent are practising the violence of retribution and retaliation. It has become central to their character structure. The sense that it is justified, a settling of old scores, can have the same sort of support of a sector of the community as the Afghan has from his whole group in settling the next stage of a blood feud. The crime may be committed with 'a good conscience', with a clear sense that it ought, justly, to be done. But, since the victims now are not the same people as committed the first assault, in so far as an 'Adult' is present, there is bound to be also a sense of guilt. Only a severe repression can block out that fact.

The Christian counsellor knows that Christ 'takes the blame'. In the sight of God, 'there is now no blame' attaching here, as St Julian of Norwich so steadily reiterated. Christ's Cross and Passion have re-established justice in the earth. Murderers, his own murderers, are forgiven. As they drive the same nails of affliction into his own hands and feet, he prays to God the Holy Father to forgive them, as he himself does, adding, as a matter of fact, that 'they do not know what they are doing'.

The Holy One of Israel is *holy*. Holiness in the Old Testament means God's reliable presence alongside the victims of social oppression, the poor, the despised, the outcasts, and the socially aborted who are persecuted for being so vulnerable and so easily victimized. Jesus knew that his prayer was heard by the Holy One whose nature he was, by that prayer, revealing.

The manifestation of original innocence, violently invaded by the influx of the adult world's evil, has, in these protesting characters, issued in the 'phenotype' or 'manifestation' of retaliatory violence. Christ has a strangely opposite way of taking vengeance. He 'took vengeance', doing what God the Father does, by being both so good and so non-violent, even by being so weak, that he invited trespass. His vulnerability invited projection and drew upon himself a hatred displaced from elsewhere. He got himself 'crucified through weakness'. By heaping our hate obediently onto him, we angry men also find justification, right-standing and sonship.

The Obedient Focusing of Rage onto Christ Crucified

Many years ago, I met, in a friend's rectory, which he kept as a home for men discharged from prison, a young man of immense physical proportions, heavily muscled, with the broadest of shoulders. He had the stance and the look of a boxer who could floor his opponent in the first round. I heard his remarkable story.

He had 'done time' and after it had been invited to stay with my friend. He had developed a habit of climbing a narrow stairway into an attic prayer-room, sitting there to gaze at the crucifix, letting its meaning seep into his soul.

Some further undetected and unadmitted offences came to light and he was sentenced to a further period in gaol. He took in with him, in his pocket, a small crucifix. Some time later a letter arrived, asking, without explanation, for another crucifix to be sent him. When at last he was out and back home, he was asked, in passing, what became of the first crucifix. His hand reached into a pocket and drew out a few shattered pieces of wood and the twisted metal which had been the Lord's body, all that was left of the first crucifix.

He explained, in a matter-of-fact way, that he had felt cruelly provoked by a prison officer who seemed to 'have it in for him'. On the occasion of one particularly flagrant taunt he had found his right fist coming up to punch the man in the face and knock him out of action. By a miracle of inner prompting he had managed instead to force that hand into the pocket where his fingers opened just enough to grasp the crucifix. All the fury of his violent anger went into that hand. He crushed the crucifix to smithereens. The twisted fragments bore witness to the strength of his retaliatory rage. His violent anger, which had been justified enough in its way and almost certainly just also in its origins, had spent itself on the Cross of Christ, accepting the Lord's request to make him, not anyone else, the victim.

As Robert Leighton, Archbishop of Glasgow in the seventeenth century wrote to a very depressed woman, 'I bid you vent your rage into the bosom of God.' The Cross of Christ is intended to draw upon himself the righteous anger of the innocent afflicted, who could not defend themselves or retaliate sufficiently to halt the injustice at the time, and who tend, therefore, to delay and inevitably to displace the reaction, so that other, relatively or totally innocent people suffer. Christ was crucified in order that now our anger can spend itself, obediently and in faith, hurting the one provided, the Lamb of God. Sin becomes 'not believing in Jesus', not trusting him to take it, and in taking it, take it away.

Religious people, who are so often depressed, are as trespassed upon as the violent victims, but the violence of their retaliatory rage is muted and turned back upon themselves. They were, and still are, in mortal terror of the consequences of letting it out. There is, as Jesus saw so clearly, a murder of the innocent child at the heart of the religious character. Rather than vent the anger on the offending parent, and knowing of no substitute being offered, they 'bite back at themselves', being filled with, *and clinging to* remorse and guilt.

Violent people who retaliate refuse, at that deep level, to accuse their foetal self or lie about its hardships and hurts. Worshipping, as one might say, 'the trickster', they pretend to take it lying down. But secretly they reserve the right to get their own back later. 'You wait, you bitch; I'll get you; just you wait,' is commonly heard, particularly in the reliving of traumatic births.

Two thieves who had committed murder were being crucified on a Friday morning. Their displaced vengeance had caught up with itself in the retributive vengeance of the law. They were not, however, at the centre of that day's work. Their companion on the central Cross had 'done nothing amiss'. He had 'gone about doing good'. Still, in this place, he was available as the one alongside. His presence and his manner of suffering enabled one of the men of violence to achieve a deep level of self-awareness and recognition of Christ's quality. He asked to be remembered when Christ came into his Kingdom and was promised Paradise in a few hours' time. Repentance and forgiveness are implicit – but Christ mentions neither – only that the murderer would be with him. Suffering together, they would still be together on the other side of death.

The soldiery obediently, but perhaps letting out some viciousness necessary to get the dirty work done, nailed Jesus to his cross. As mere instruments of religious authorities whose envy and insecurity wanted him out of the way, the soldiers were excused and forgiven. It was the priests and the ecclesiastical lawyers, still entrenched behind their own basic lies, who crucified Christ and put themselves beyond the reach of his offer of forgiveness. They hated their weakness and in so doing opted out of membership of that crazy Kingdom where the king is crucified, his crown made up of thorns, and whose subjects are the despised of the earth. Or they were those rare men, like Nicodemus, ready, at first, only to come by night, but to come nevertheless. He was ready to be born again yet could not understand what that meant, until his fears fell from him just at the point when the paraded disciples were taking to their heels.

Pastoral care and counselling must address itself to the violent youth of our times. They are not, as I see them, rampaging pointlessly, so much as retaliating by symbolic acts against primal injuries done to them at the beginning. We must begin, not with the law or talk about social responsibility. Such talk cannot reach to the whereabouts and context of their hurt. What does reach down, to alter the hurt experience, is the Cross and Passion of Christ. This man Jesus died, rose from the dead and is with us now. His Holy Spirit can and does apply his transforming work at the proper depth. We now understand that psychodynamic depth of origin to be as early as the first trimester of life in the womb.

Prevention

Among other things it is prevention we must plan for. It has been the charge against pastoral counsellors for many years that we have been high on our attempts to cure or alleviate the distress of our clients but low on any attempts to think through and educate even our own folk in styles of living that would ensure less victims, less neurosis and less personality and character disorder.

I think now that there was some sense in our reluctance in earlier years to stick our necks out as though we knew how to deal with the roots of violence. We knew enough to know that we did not know where the tap root of the trauma was or where the whole angry reaction lay in our developmental history. The maternal-foetal distress syndrome that I have offered here as the hermeneutical or interpretative principle for our understanding of the origins of disorders characterized by violence, not only accounts for the strange details of the syndrome; but it also matches and correlates with the detail of the redemptive identification of Jesus Christ with our race in God's supreme act of love, justice and power. The Cross of Christ, offered in depth at the point of primal impact, offers immense prophylactic possibilities. The violence emerges partly from anger at the intolerable isolation and partly from the evil input which is so hard to bear alone. Christ overcomes the isolation, shares in minute detail the form of the three-fold affliction, and in so doing makes it bearable. Above all, he refuses to blame. We sin now *when we cling* to self-blame, preferring it to his blameless company. We sin *when we let the blame of others stick*, nursing the grievance, rather than firmly drawing their attention to the blamelessness that is ours in Christ, on God's authority.

Agreeing then, with Hans Krebs that the most likely candidate among the external causes of the violent character is the change in the patterns and aspirations of women about to become and becoming mothers, we must in all fairness recognize that this is itself a change brought about in women and wives by the failure of husbands to initiate a strong and protective love, really embracing their wives. We men could have prayed for the power to embody God's initiating love, modelled on Christ's love for the Church. But mostly we did not and I among them. It is as plain as could be that Christ's love for the Church is not based on her attractiveness or unspoiled beauty. God is not put off, disappointed, nor does he stop loving the Church on account of any deficiency. Nor should a man be 'fastidious' about his wife. His is *a covenant love* sustained by a covenant-keeping God.

Of course we shall be keen to honour the work of the neo-Freudians in their insistence on Mother-Baby bonding from birth onward. Bowlby, Winnicott, the Robertsons, Fairbairn, Guntrip and Balint, to mention only those whose writings have influenced psychiatry, social work and counselling in England, have an unassailed case. So has Dr Frederic Leboyer in pressing for a gentler midwifery. Their arguments, that we should give priority to the sanctity of the bond between mother and baby are far from being heard in many of our most prestigious hospitals, though perhaps the tide is turning.

If, however, our attention is focused on the reduction of violence in personality, it would seem to be more profitable to pay more respect to the maternal-foetal relationship within the first trimester after conception, and throughout life in the womb.

Testing the Hypothesis

If all that has been advanced here about the origins of the violent character disorders is tested, as any hypothesis should be, the findings and results of 'therapy', 're-education' or 'reappraisal' will eventually nullify it or leave it the stronger. That could bring in a verdict quite soon.

Whether there are observable differences between the characters of those whose mothers were distressed in the first trimester and those who were happy then can also be the subject of testing now. If, in the light of these findings (should they establish the hypothesis, by leaving it intact and not nullifying it), the pattern of employing pregnant women and keeping them externally busy as if nothing significant has happened should change we should enable them to adjust peacefully to the mothering role.

We would, of course, have to wait for a couple of decades before we knew for certain that intra-uterine 'violence' had led to adolescent violence in such a way that the reduction of the one reduced the other. The other ways of testing the hypothesis are in establishing whether violence had been done to the mother, which distressed her in the first trimester of this man's pregnancy, and by pre-natal integration work as he remembers whether his intra-uterine response led to recognizable violent reactions.

However, Christians and humanists who are sensitive to these issues, may well respond now to this finding. They will attach importance from the onset of pregnancy, indeed before it is planned, to the mother's emotional health and tranquillity. Since this tranquillity and supportedness depend largely on her husband, family and neighbourhood contacts, these too will become consciously significant. If some must live surrounded by concrete walls, would days in the country help, or just provoke resentment? Who knows?

To summarize: there is evidence to show that violence done to the mother, of whatever kind and degree, will distress her. Her distress is shared by the foetus. This maternal-foetal distress, both the impact on the foetus of being 'marinated' in her miseries, and the foetal reactions which are so varied, tend to become the self's way of experiencing itself and perceiving both its cosmos and its core for the rest of life. It affects most powerfully what can be believed, at heart and in 'the guts', about justice in the universe, about God and man, as well as about institutions. It affects all groups in which individuals can be 'homogenized'. It projects onto the family and pervades all intimate relationships.

Non-violence *then*, ensured by a priority given to the love and care of pregnant women, to providing understanding, expressive, genuine, and respectful relationships would, I believe, be the best preventive we know of, to cut back on our at present monstrous production of violent young persons. The past two decades have seen a true increase of tenderness between mothers and babies from birth onwards. The sense that they are, from birth, small persons, human beings who respond best when treated as such, is more generally accepted. Birth is better understood and more wisely written about than ever before. Mothers want and are ready for more than many of our hospitals can yet give in safe and sensitive obstetrics.

In this matter of first trimester tranquillity, we do not need to wait for professionals to approve of the changes we wish to make, nor depend on them to 'service' our efforts. It is open to any married couple to respond to this insight and act accordingly.

When God the Holy Father's plan for the conception and growth of his Son in the womb of a virgin was getting under way, he foresaw Joseph's response to this shocking and unprecedented event. The Annunciation, the special preparatory message, was, in a sense, the pre-pregnancy counselling of the Blessed Virgin Mary. These reassuring, prophetic words equipped her to accept and endure what was to follow. In her first trimester, with Jesus in her womb, the discovery of the pregnancy opened up a period of intense insecurity. Joseph was a just man but even he was minded to put her away on the quiet. Had he not been merciful there was a risk of total disgrace, humiliation, even of false accusation and worse. The adulteress could be stoned to death. The empathy of the Annunciation, acknowledging Mary's inevitable fear and then calming her with the promises of God, could well be a model for us.

I am particularly concerned for those, especially among Christian readers, who may be angry and incensed that this places yet another responsibility on parents, rather than beating the more popular drum of the duties of children to their parents. I can beat that too, and will, with conviction of its equal rightness on some other occasion. Those who have themselves suffered intra-uterine distress, but rallied to defend their mothers, then and since, will tend to be most angry.

If *we* have ever known anxiety-depression this is a clue, I believe, to the same problem of violence. There is violence in the way we drive ourselves to work for our acceptance. We are the religious whose violence has always been retroflected. It is in our clenched teeth, through which we struggle, nevertheless, to produce faint smiles, to cover up the hostility we cannot admit to. For us, the cure, which the overtly violent can find in Christ, is concealed by our guile. We have a two-stage journey to the foot of the Cross. They are already there. Our existence, occupying pews, claiming to represent Christ, is perhaps the greatest block to their recognizing him and what he can do for them.

What I have written has focused upon the pastoral counselling of a category of sufferers, the violent, who as yet seldom come our way (unless we are youth-club leaders, community workers, police, probation officers, or work with prisoners or for their after-care). I trust that they will come to themselves and to Christ.

Restraint Is not an Adequate Answer

When once the violence has been painfully and ruthlessly imprinted, the dynamics of retaliation are established and fixated. They lurk in the shadows. The least hint of injustice in contemporary life can trigger off the primal violence. The victim's reason is clouded. He cannot see that to switch roles is a poor answer. To add another innocent victim to the pile, so far from putting the wrong to rights, compounds the worst evil of it. But pain and humiliation blunt the conscience, justifying personal vengeance and caring nothing that it is displaced onto someone not dimly connected with the offence. Restraining measures are not easily developed and may fail.

The remedial structures are in emotionally costly, godly (that is, 'God-like') parenting, schooling, befriending and community caring backed up by just laws justly administered. This may well be sufficient to reduce the anger, relax the rage, and turn aside or simply not arouse the streak of violent acting-out.

Restraint, however, is not cure. Nothing radical has been done to heal the memories of violent assault and vile penetration, by promulgating ordinary law or even extraordinary love.

It is not glib to assert that making God's kingly rule evident in the middle of murderous, vicious violence is uniquely Christ's work. His Cross and suffering mediate forgiveness and proclaim a new state of affairs between God and man and between human beings. This new world of relationships, which the person who has turned to Christ with the obedience of faith has entered, is a new creation all round him. It comes to birth and life also within the believer and is the fellowship of love that believers constitute.

* 'Mayhem': used here in a general sense; specifically it means 'the crime of maiming a person so as to make him less able to defend himself or annoy his adversary' (*Shorter Oxford English Dictionary*).

CHAPTER 10

The Pastoral Understanding of Homosexuality

Sex as a Problem

It is impossible for me to write about tight corners in counselling without admitting how little help I have had, and how little help at times I have been able to give, when the patient's difficulty is a dilemma about the place of sexuality in the Christian life.

Christianity is rightly and necessarily accused in the twentieth century, and not for the first time, of turning sex into a problem. Christianity is incurably ethical. Its moral requirements confine genital-sexual intercourse to the sole, often sexually ill-adjusted relationship of marriage. Such restraints become irksome. As painful obstacles to the legitimized pleasure of almost every kind of sexual activity, the Church's moral restraints have become themselves regarded as immoral, suppressive and wrong when measured against the standards of this age.

Having turned sex into a problem, Christian guides have often failed to give 'humane' answers. As Søren Kierkegaard wrote:

> The whole question about the significance of the sexual and its significance in the particular spheres has undeniably been poorly answered until now, and above all it is very seldom answered with the right feeling. To utter witticisms about it is a lowly art, to admonish is not difficult, to preach about it in such a way as to leave out the difficulties is not hard to do, but to talk about it in a fashion truly humane is an art.[1]

Pastoral counsellors may be indebted to recent books by Roman

[1] S. Kierkegaard, *The Concept of Dread* (Princeton, Princeton University Press), 1944.

Catholic authors who have courageously tackled thorny aspects of sexual ethics, particularly problems about homosexuality.[2,3] To be prepared to discuss these subjects arouses a fiercely dangerous set of emotions, bent on the suppression even of fair discussion. I hesitate myself to enter this arena of powerful emotional identifications, because it is hard to do so without seeming to take sides. Though I never find myself in a tight corner in working with men and women with problems of same-sex loving, it is difficult to negotiate a passage in the jostling crowd of partisans who are only too ready to condemn their opponents.

There is a guilt of association which fastens upon those who are known to counsel people in sexual difficulties. This presupposes their shared activity as being somehow sinful. Counsellor and client must surely both be tinged with guilt? Counsellors are felt to be suspiciously curious. Are they not giving way to some evil fascination? Are they getting sick thrills themselves by proxy? By what right do they revise society's safe rule of thumb, by which all sexual 'deviants' should be ostracized? In the stern mind of the critics, aberrant or unruly sexuality is never a burden which can be shared. It is, rather, a 'mark of the beast', sufficient to identify a shameless sinner who must be driven out of the society of decent people.

Some people who have been party to some witch-hunts of homosexuals in particular in their earlier years, have themselves in middle age suffered from breakdowns and have come for help. They have come to an increasing self-awareness and deepening insight into their own darker nature. They realize that this was rigorously repressed in their youth. Now in their riper years they are able to open it up to consciousness and accept it as part of their own immature drives. They can assimilate it as an aspect of their total self-hood. To be able to include the dangerously bad in their own lives, in this retrospective accounting, and share it with others, is possible only when the sharing relationship, with an individual or with a group, has become strong enough to bear it.

To their chagrin, as they look back, they recognize that in fiercely persecuting the sexual deviant, and in working to have him put away out of sight and out of mind, they have been scapegoating him. They have been attributing to him their own secret and unadmitted desires. With a strange hectic excitement they have la-

[2] D. Goergen, *The Sexual Celibate*, SPCK 1976.
[3] J. J. McNeill, *The Church and the Homosexual*. Darton, Longman and Todd, 1977.

belled him as the evil one they cannot admit themselves to being. Having this deviant ceremonially driven away into the wilderness felt cathartic, as if the scapegoater was himself purged. He felt wonderfully cleansed from defilement. But this was a mistaken projection from within himself to outside himself. He has displaced, from his own guilty self, his fear of exposure, loss of face and loss self-esteem. They have been put on to the scapegoat. The disgrace of the scapegoat was precisely the disgrace the persecutor unconsciously feared would be his own hard lot. Insightful recollection enables former scapegoaters to own their own deviance.

It is the task of pastoral counsellors (and this includes all those who write about sexual issues) to stand alongside those who are scapegoated. Christ identified himself with the scurrilous and socially deviant. Those who claim they care seldom say 'Come unto me' to such people, but there are some who do. They may be abused for doing so, just as Christ was. The sequel is a shared sense of having come to terms with the reality of suffering and sin which is what 'bearing the cross' is about. It becomes the ground of our growing conviction that Jesus was exactly correct when he made the unusual assertion that to 'be persecuted', for relating rightly to him and to his scapegoated friends, is to be blessed, and to be really happy. We miss the blessing if we forget the promise and resent the persecution.

There is less prejudice when a secular, psychiatrically trained pastoral counsellor is known to be working with homosexuals than when it is a clergyman. Fr McNeill quotes the report of the National Federation of Priests' Councils in the USA. 'Individual priests and ministers, working with homosexuals, usually encounter a social and psychological stigma as a result of their work, and this stigma is the single most effective obstacle to ministers who want to work with homosexuals.'[4]

There has been a falling off in the number of homosexual clergymen and teachers who have come to me for counselling since the view began to be accepted that homosexual preference is in no sense abnormal, but simply a variation of the human sexual pattern which in the majority is to be heterosexual. So I am surprised that in this climate Fr McNeill should write, 'Practically all authorities agree that the first goal of counselling should be to guide the person with

[4] Ibid., pp. 155-6.

a homosexual problem to a heterosexual adjustment whenever possible.' In support, he quotes the officers of a major homophile
organization, the Mattachine Society, as agreeing with this aim:

> On the basis of our experience – the embarrassment, shame, and
> humiliation so many of us have known – we would definitely
> advise anyone who has not yet become an active homosexual, but
> has only misgivings about himself, to go the other way if he can.[5]

This advice is given because of the mental pain of 'coming out'
as a homosexual in a society which can still be savagely prejudiced.
My own comment on this, based on several thousands of hours in
depth counselling of men and women with homophilia and hetero-
phobia (love of their own sex and fear of, or shrinking from, sexual
commitment to the opposite sex) is that even in a loving and
accepting social group, they encounter, within their own basic relationship to themselves, an often savage and persistent self-hatred,
self-scorn, a self-punitive, self-humiliating and self-destructive impulse.

These self-deprecating dynamics and the sense of being ashamed
of the self, tend to alternate with the equally common male homosexual feeling that, in the face of intolerable, crushing, destructive
and annihilating forces, he has to show immense courage. Under
persecution in this blind, relentless, pitiless, humiliating and de-
grading world, he had to behave as a hero. In the face of the enmity
of the woman's clumsy invasive and expulsive forces, he had to be
able to look after himself. In the reliving of their births there is
often a clear recognition by such men that the 'enemy' was the
woman. The closest woman, the mother, was transformed by the
brute forces of labour and her difficult passages into a permanent
source of terror. Only his own kind are reliable. (The analogous
situation, when the foetus is female, leads to a common enough
personality reaction pattern of man-centred, woman-hating hysteria, the *grande hysterique* among women: the bane of the male
counsellor's life until he becomes their match by skill and love.)
The male foetus grows to need the help of men to face the persecuting world of hostile, often feminine, forces.

The deeply caring, secure, intimate world of integrative therapy
makes these projections of hostility on to women unrealistic. The

[5] Ibid., pp. 156.

homosexual begins to face at source some of the primal experiences of which both his self-scorn and his self-admiration are later life expressions.

This way of accounting for the homosexual condition has led me to the view (shared by all the primal therapists I know) that the profound distaste for women at close quarters, the heroic proportions of the self, and the focusing of hysterical and jealous love upon men – which are common both to male homosexuals and to the analogous male-clinging women (but not to lesbians) – are direct consequences of foetal and peri-natal damage.

Our Latest Views on Psychogenesis – 1977–80

There has been great progress in our research findings, accelerating over the past three years, since we permitted ourselves to look into the first trimester and the maternal-foetal distress syndrome. It has always been apparent to me that the well-defended man who, to the 'civilized' Western way of being human, is a 'normal' man, who is also homosexual, is 'normal' and well defended in exactly the same way as the schizoid personality. Both are defended, the main difference being that the homosexual man has the advantage, or misfortune (depending on how you look at it), of being eagerly open to, and not in a schizoid way defended against, the intimate love of a man. About women he is typically schizoid, experiencing discomfort at physical intimacy with them. 'Intimacy', in this context, does not mean genital sexual congress but long-term bondedness in a close and interdependent relationship. If that is so, it follows that insofar as we are now looking confidently at the first trimester for the origins of schizoid affliction, *it is to the same first trimester that we will look to discover the origins of homosexuality in men and possibly also in women*. Their schizoid or afflicted aspects, wary of intimacy with women and sick at the thought of being inside their bodies, their unstable self-evaluation, with mixed narcissism and self-scorn, are readily assimilated to what we have already written in Chapter 2 about the origins of schizoid dynamics.

Why Such Heart-ache?

The question arises, why, in association with feelings of intense distress and revulsion at being both invaded and surrounded by so much female misery, there should also be this heartache for the intimate love of a man. The answer, given at this moment of the reliving of experience early in the womb, by a sufficient number of homosexual men (and by others in whom the yearning has been, until this occasion of reliving, fully repressed) *is that this yearning is a result of the transfusion of exactly that state of mind and emotional longing in the mother, from her to the foetus, through the foeto-placental circulation.*

Both Freud and Fenichel[6] associated male homosexuality with weak or absent fathers, as well as with weak or absent mothers. Freud made the suggestion that the extent of male homosexuality in ancient Greece may have been due to the fact that children were brought up by male slaves. By contrast, Clifford Allen[7] suggested that the widespread homosexuality of the East may be due to the fact that the child is brought up in the harem until puberty and has few male contacts. 'Identifying himself with women he feels himself feminine and can love only males.' In the matter of explanations of the origin of 'gay' love based on post-natal influencing, either 'You pays your money and you takes your choice', or 'Heads I win, tails you lose'. Without denying that childhood conditioning has reinforcing or inhibiting effects, our evidence points to the relevance of the Freud-Fenichel observations about weak and emotionally or actually absent fathers, and mothers also, *not in its post-natal but in its pre-natal causality, in fact, as part of the maternal-foetal distress syndrome.* The mother herself is no more or less than a healthy woman with normal longings if, when she discovers that she is now a pregnant mother, she turns to her husband with an increased need of his protective, supporting, sharing, understanding and more-generously-giving love and caring. If she has, in her own personality, elements of inadequacy, all the more does the discovery of pregnancy press her towards feelings of increased dependency. This will be expressed in a greater expectation or demand for the husband's closeness, time, attention, self-giving and care. Even women who later decide, when disappointed by their men-folk, to go it alone and be 'strong' and independent, if only to diminish the pain of constant let-down by the husband, can often recall a time when they still hoped, indeed yearned for the intimate, reliable, strong, readily available and summonable support of a real husband, instead of a frightened rabbit, a thick-hided hippo, or a startled bird

[6] Otto Fenichel, *The Psychoanalytic Theory of Neurosis*, Routledge & Kegal Paul, 1946.
[7] Clifford Allen, *A Textbook of Psychosexual Disorders*, Oxford University Press, 1962.

always on the point of flying away to be at peace, anywhere but where she is.

It is this *combination of the mother's emotional distress at her life situation plus her yearning for the intimate love of her man* that are transferred into and impressed upon the foetus, early in intra-uterine life. What is crucial to this hypothesis is the recognition, by the adult, while reliving the foetal experience, of this combination of feelings (with others often surprisingly added) so familiar to them, and their own correlating of the paired experiences. It is effective when the man can say, with conviction, that in essence, 'These are not my feelings, they are my mother's. With no thanks for the loan, I return them to her.' If they have served the mysterious purposes of God, there may even be praise for them, but that is another matter.

The subject then has to face the quite immense task of rolling up his stair-carpet, now loose at the bottom, only to find it tacked or nailed down hard by the same-shaped nails, at each developmental stair through life. Each step of the Eriksonian stairway has been distorted and rendered insecure for the growing boy by the fixated persistence of the maternal-foetal distress syndrome. It has distorted his perception either by interposing schizoid aversions when he has looked at women, and at times at the whole cosmos, or it has done this by interposing an hysterical yearning for men, equivalent to his mother's for her husband, whose indispensability as a rescuer is only matched by his predictable betrayal and evasiveness.

Each step of development has to be gone over again, revising it in the light of the new basic understanding that 'I had become, in a sense, "possessed" by my mother's emotions during our most intimately shared months, at my point of maximum impression-ability.' But since the original impression on the wax of the organism is now manifest, the task can go on unhindered by delaying tugs on the sleeve by previous encounters that have been overlooked.

The Lesbian Lock

What of Lesbian tendencies, the equivalent powerful addiction in women to the love of persons of their own sex? Is it not absurd to posit, in a woman who has just discovered (or not yet discovered) that she is pregnant, a fierce desire to be close, not to her husband, but to some woman or other?

It is by no means absurd. Indeed the shock of pregnancy in an immature or emotionally fixated woman commonly does precipitate a regression. The 'leaving' of home and mother and 'cleaving' to the husband has never been satisfactorily concluded. The fear of the unknown makes her feel 'all child' again, and the mother's closeness is emotionally demanded. The husband fades into relative insignificance. However we portray to ourselves the complex emotions of such a woman during the first and subsequent trimesters, we envisage them as infiltrating and taking over the foetus, unless it has already developed a healthy capacity to protest and combat this humiliating dependency on the woman.

An example from our integration workshops: a young professional woman in a very disturbed state was referred to us by a clinical psychologist. She had become enamoured of and captivated by an older woman who had Lesbian tendencies but who was not prepared to 'come out' and join her in a publicly recognizable relationship. The stop-go moves of the friend so disturbed her that she could not work, became actively suicidal, on several occasions slashing her wrists (a typical attack on the bloody cord) and was unable to eat, losing weight in severe anorexia.

In course of integration work, which she was readily able to do, she became aware, while focusing on the first trimester, of an overwhelming longing surging through her, which she recognized as not hers but 'from out there', for the closeness of some all-important woman. The all-or-nothing intensity of this painful yearning she herself recognized (since, of course, there is no question of interpretation here, our role is simply facilitative) as identical in force, direction and urgency to her feelings for the elusive woman friend.

Baffled as to the possible source of this intense fixation, she asked her parents about their feelings during her mother's pregnancy, to be told of the terrible distress of the mother during those months. The father's work had moved the family from the place where the mother's one-and-only precious woman friend still lived. Without her she was absolutely inconsolable and the new home a dungeon. The father wryly reported that as far as his wife was concerned, the one thing wrong with their honeymoon was that this very special woman friend could not be there with them. The link was unmistakable.

Obviously, where there is such severity of maternal-foetal distress, leading to displacement of the negative umbilical affect into the alimentary tract, with the typical symbolic refusal of input that leads to anorexia nervosa, the therapeutic task ranges much further than the elucidation of her lesbian fixation by 'handing it back to the mother'. All the years during which she should have been becoming aware of her own needs, as her psycho-sexual development proceeded, they had been totally taken over by the overpowering and pervasive force of the mother's neurotic fixation. To go back over those years with the bottom step of the stair-carpet freed, to loosen it all the way up and then to relay it with an unworn tread or lay down something quite different, is a major task.

This is not the place to detail the very thorough steps we take to ensure that the potential freedom gained by the discoveries and reconciliations of pre-natal and peri-natal integration work becomes actual and progressively usable as the months go by. Some return for week-ends when they can 'swap hours' and facilitate one another, hosted by our house team who have had much experience of the work.

The house-team themselves discovered the value, for this forward revision, of our second-year, five-day residential seminar. This long-standing course takes the student through each of the Eriksonian stages of development with experiential learning methods in each three-hour session. They found that to take a close look again at their adolescence, for instance, subtracting from it the misperceptions they had been inadvertently employing at the time, so tending to project constricting and invading behaviour on to their parents, to which 'attack' they had over-reacted, gave them a new view of their parents and themselves during this transition. They realized how much better it could have been without their projected hostility. This re-evaluation also led to a clear sense that they would have broken away to freedom then, had they not made the first priority ensuring that mother should not be distressed, obliterating their own legitimate needs by so doing.

I conclude that though the psychogenic roots of homosexuality in men and women in the first trimester can now be taken as a workable hypothesis, rooted in and related to the maternal-foetal distress syndrome, the dynamics of each person are quite individual and specific. They will certainly have gathered later determinants in subsequent trimesters, in difficult births and in all the successive stages of psycho-sexual development. The important task for psycho-pathological research has always been to determine the origins. These findings seem to do that.

The hypothesis is nullified if there should be, over a series of well-investigated cases with reasonably informative parents, no significant correlation between the feelings and background emotional colouring and the sexual drive of the subject with that of his mother, overt or suppressed, in the early months of the pregnancy.

It would also be nullified if pre-natal integration work did not lead to a reliving of the complained-of symptoms, the schizoid aversions and hysterical yearnings, when focusing on the first trimester. So far, the hypothesis has not been nullified on either count.

I am not well informed as to research in animals. It would be surprising if no studies had been done on the effect of stress applied to pregnant mammals on the behaviour and psychological reactions of their offspring. I am open to information on this point.

The Successful Lie

It is often said that the opinion of someone like myself, who tends to see at depth only the sad, troubled, sick and avowedly needy and ill-adjusted members of the homophile community, is irrelevant as an account of the psychological origins of well-adjusted, frankly successful, socially competent homosexual men. They are so happy in each other, there can surely be nothing wrong or pathological in the 'gay' couples engaged in same-sex loving? That could be so. But I think it is not, for the following reasons. The adjustment of individuals to contemporary Western society is itself achieved only at the expense of considerable repression, denial of weakness and of primal catastrophe. Adjustment, as Ernest Becker shows brilliantly, demands the repression of fears of death itself at the beginning and at the end of life. 'What we call the human character is actually a lie about the nature of reality.'[8] Becker cites Otto Rank:

> 'Man is the more normal, healthy or happy, the more he can . . . successfully . . . repress, displace, deny, rationalize, dramatize himself and deceive others.' Human character is a 'vital lie'; the more stable the character the more successful the lie.[9]

[8] E. Becker, *The Denial of Death*. Collier Macmillan, 1973.
[9] O. Rank, *Will Therapy and Truth and Reality*, pp. 251–2; and Becker, op. cit.

By contrast, the neurotic person suffers because he or she cannot maintain intact all the defence mechanisms which come to the aid of those who are better able to adjust to the illusions, false goals and systematized deceptions of Western culture. So Rank claimed; and so, in agreement, does Becker. I too hold that:

> Spiritually the neurotic has been long since where psychoanalysis wants to bring him without being able to, namely at the point of seeing through the deception of the world of sense, the falsity of reality. The refusal of his defence mechanisms to ward off the pain . . . robs him of the illusions important for living . . . He is much nearer to the actual truth psychologically than the others and it is just that from which he suffers.[10]

We ought not to invalidate our findings because they have been gathered from the direct reliving and re-experiencing of those homo-sexuals who have encountered their symptoms as painful and dis-tressing and not cases gathered from well-adjusted members of that group. As with all the other personality types, it is only when for some reason or other the individual, willingly, or more often un-willingly, finds that the foundations of his or her personality are laid open, that we are able to build up a valid picture of the origins of particular character-types.

It is considerations such as these which put me at variance with the view now often advanced by the homophile organizations, that the homosexual character orientations are entirely healthy. They insist that the desire for marital-like intimacy and genital union with one's own sex is a variant of normal development which is perfectly natural and acceptable, whether or not it leads to genital-sexual encounters, for a significantly large minority of men and women in Western society.

Later Intra-Uterine Experience

I have other tentative explanations in addition to those given above of homosexual dynamic origins, arising out of research that has been going on for twenty-five years. At first it seemed that difficult births were to be seen as the first conditioning event that turned the baby (whether boy or girl) decisively away from trust in the

[10] E. Becker, op. cit.

woman who, as we have seen in previous chapters, is experienced as an overbearing, crushing or suffocating force. In most recent years the imprint of life in the womb on subsequent character development has become much clearer to us. Ten or more years ago I wrote, in a pamphlet on 'Identity':

> Undoubtedly there is a kind of identity imprinted on the mind by the experience of the baby in the womb. One could express it in the phrase, 'I am happy, content, curled up and cosy, with nothing at all to bother about, no changes in environment, no threat of any kind to this primitive mode of existence.'[11]

That I now know to be by no means universal. As a generalization it is naïve and inaccurate. The work of Francis Mott points to memories of centrally significant, good and bad, experiences in the interaction of the mother and of the foetus during the forty weeks of the pregnancy. What passes to and fro through the umbilical cord is of the utmost importance, not just as to the passage of the necessary nutrients, but as to powerful emotional messages from the mother about what is going on inside her. We inquire about the actual or likely effect of the growing foetus on her well-being, on her ability to cope with life and to enjoy it. Knowing as we do what mixed emotions, indeed what totally opposite emotions, from early loathing to eventual longing, women commonly feel for the foetus growing within them, the effect of the fluctuating inconstancy can be very unsettling.

Moreover we are gaining a much clearer sense of the way in which the foetus can have fantasies of relating, via the umbilical cord, with its spread-out roots in the placenta embedded in the ground of the maternal womb. A wide range of fantasies attribute powers to the placenta, both for good and ill, for protecting the foetus or itself needing to be protected. It is felt as both attacking and attacked, as siding with the foetus against the 'bad mother' or with the 'bad mother' against the foetal self. For Mott, this was common, for us it is unusual.

Freud speculated on mythological twin symbolism in a letter to Jung in 1911, and hinted at the importance of the placenta. He suggested, citing the care given to the afterbirth in certain primitive peoples, that the placenta is the weaker twin, who dies first. Jung

[11] F. Lake, *Identity*. CTA Pamphlet, 1970.

found this suggestion 'extraordinarily interesting' and replied to Freud that 'there are things whose only explanation is intra-uterine.'[12] Jung felt that such early memories are not individual but psychogenetic. I would question that opinion, since I believe that these intra-uterine affects are widely different, and are therefore individual memories. I have reason to confirm those early speculations of Freud and Jung from the experience of primal work.

Some men with fixated homosexual preferences have reported relating with intense concern to their 'brother the placenta'. Together they have been in league against the monstrous regiment of the overbearing maternal world. They have been astonished at recognizing that their fixated bereavement for this brother placenta when it 'died' at their birth, had powerfully motivated their search for a successor to this understanding partner – of somewhat indefinable sex, but in fantasy the same as their own.

There are, of course, other explanations of homosexual inclination from later stages of life. When we are not able to handle our lives competently in the here-and-now, at our actual age level, we tend to regress to an earlier age. We begin to experience life on an earlier level and try to solve our present-day problems with the emotional equipment of that earlier age range. So a young adult man or woman can regress to the latency period (approximately five to twelve years) when it is perfectly normal to be wanting a 'chum' of one's own age and sex to do exciting things with; or for a boy to be wanting a father, or a girl a mother, to go together with on adventures of discovery. Not recognizing what is happening, the time-displaced adult can be scared of the homosexuality, which is in fact a normal and necessary stage of development, even though more applicable to that earlier age to which he has regressed. It is even more seductive and distressing if a person spent those latency years longing for a friend or a parent whom he never really had. Harry Stack Sullivan found, and many agree with him, that early sexual maturation, or early puberty in a boy, who has not found such a friend or not been able to work through a good relationship with an accessible father, tends to produce an overlap which is disastrous to the female-object search. It perpetuates the friend-seeking, or father-seeking phase at a time when genital dynamisms are already in full flood.

[12] *Freud-Jung Letters* Nos 274, 275. October 1911. The Hogarth Press and Routledge & Kegan Paul, 1974.

An even deeper regression can take the adult into a babyhood in which he had turned against his mother, who was busy with the new baby, and attached himself to his father with immense devotion, tenderness, and demonstrative affection.

Learning to Love

I was once asked to help a young man in his early twenties who was troubled by the realization that he did not feel that strong desire for a growing intimate friendship with a woman that would lead him to suppose that one day he could marry. On the contrary he had unpleasant feelings of wanting urgently to get away whenever a woman seemed to want to establish a more loving and intimate relationship.

Baffled by these powerful revulsions to women, he wondered whether he was incapable of relating in loving intimacy with anyone. Then he picked up an article written by a homosexual clergyman and immediately began to wonder whether he was perhaps fated never to have a wife or children or grandchildren, or a home within which his sexual nature could be properly expressed. Was he one of the homosexual minority? He felt isolated, horrified and guilty. However, he let his fantasies experiment with the idea of tender relationships with men of his own age and found less fear and resistance than occurred when he fantasied about women. Then he got into a relationship with a fellow-student who had had a good deal of homosexual experience. This man persuaded him that he should come out of his lonely guilt and join the homosexual community.

But there was something about the attitudes of this homosexual group towards women, towards family life, and towards people who were moving in or towards heterosexual relationships, that seemed stridently scornful and unconstructively negative. It was one thing to draw men, who felt lonely and guilty about something they were totally innocent of, into a fellowship and out of loneliness. But why this aggressive mono-sexuality? Why love only men? Would this new mono-sexual minority community he had been invited to join ever accept a place in a wider society, even if it were offered? Was it rather a collective of guilt, brazening itself out, striving to normalize itself by taking over a place in the media? It did not feel as healthy or as happy as it tried to make out.

Then he looked again at what the Church offered him, because he had been converted to Christ at a camp in his early teens. He was still attending church but had gone into his shell and had drawn away from any thought of being frank about his feelings for men, because of things he had heard the vicar say. This rigid clergyman was vicious and scornful in his denunciation of sexual offenders, with a special 'down' on homosexuals. He could never talk to him, or in any group where his influence presided.

Then he was asked to go to a group for prayer and Bible study. The man who asked him had a kind of depth about him which encouraged confidence, so he went. There was some sharing of personal problems and one of the group, obviously respected and loved by the others, spoke of some healing of the memories which had delivered him of a life-long fear of closeness to women. He said, quite at ease, 'I can understand how I came to believe I was homosexual. I could love men tenderly, and a woman too, until I began to get too burdened with her expectations. It was the fear of prolonged closeness that made me sheer away from women. It was my mother I was scared of, even though she was a good woman.'

To find a Christian group in which he knew he could speak openly about sexuality and its problems led to a request for some guidance as to how he could better handle this element in his personality. Already it had been reduced in size from a mountain about to crush him totally to being just one of many problems which he could discuss with friends in Christ, as a whole person who was wholly accepted. This young man learned much in his prayer group about 'walking in the light, and having fellowship and letting the blood of Christ deal with sin' (I John 1:7). What more could one say to him about the subject of homosexuality, about the capacity to love, even the preference for loving people of one's own sex?

The pastoral counsellor needs to recognize that the label 'homosexual' is an emotive one. It means, in one sense of course, a lover of one's own sex, with erotic attraction as an adult, one who is wholly or partially inhibited in loving persons of the opposite sex. But we must also recognize that it means many things at once — both good and bad, healthy and sick, mature and immature, virtuous and sinful, constructive and destructive. To use it accurately, as a stereotype for a group of people who are to be exalted or

abased, approved of, tolerated or knocked down, only adds confusion and misunderstanding.

If the personality problem the client is wrestling with is made up
of fears of commitment to women and a strangely compulsive need
for a commitment to men, with a deep fear of losing their friendship,
the pastoral counsellor can start by helping the client not to fear
this, but to accept it as a part of the human base line from which
to work. It helps to convey to the client the sense that there is a
positive healthy love for one's own sex, based on a capacity for deep
and intimate friendship between fathers and sons. That must follow
wherever, for instance, a baby boy has been tenderly loved by his
father who has taken over the nursing from mother. For ever afterwards he has a strong reciprocal feeling of love towards fatherly
men. Cultural conditioning in Germany, England and the United
States has attempted to eradicate this mutual tenderness between
men. But where the Holy Spirit is at work this fear-laden taboo on
tenderness between men is lifted. A strong, wholly good love
emerges.

Men who are scared of this normal healthy aspect of homosexual
tenderness are usually out of touch with the wholesome, nurturing
feminine side of human nature. They are not able to be tender at
all. Even if they marry they remain afraid of the gentler emotions,
terrified of not being 'masculine'. Their rejection of the tender
aspects of loving, either towards men or women, is sick. The positive, deeply affectionate loving and holding of persons of one's own
sex, without needing genital excursions, is entirely healthy.

Pastoral counselling can help the client recognize and be sensitive
to the boundary between this deep affectionate friendship in Christ,
and genital sexuality. No question of sin arises if we are referring
to these wider aspects of loving. It is the genital aspect which easily
gets out of proportion.

I used to use public opinion as the criterion for the acceptability
or not of our secret fantasy life and the acted-out behaviour to
which it often leads. But that is no longer a reliable criterion. What
used to be 'shameful' is now 'shameless'. There are those who
'knowing the judgement of God' on such affairs 'not only do the
same, but have pleasure in them that do them' (Rom. 1:32 A.V.).
They now speak from within the Church. Without censure they
recommend the clubs, the organizations and agencies in which
homosexuals tend to become monosexuals, and are encouraged to

engage in genital, oral, and anal ways at arriving at orgasmic climax. The argument is that between consenting adults no one is harmed. That is not true. What a man may claim is not harmful only for so long as it is kept secret, is inevitably damaging to his integrity. He means and intends to be one thing in public and another in private. This is a harmful falsity. Those who do these things cannot expect the whole body of Christians to cut loose from the scriptures and the Spirit's age-long advice that such behaviour is a trespass, as is the trespassing of adultery and fornication.

There is an aspect of homosexuality which is the love of persons of one's own sex which is wholly creative, God-given and deeply in touch with a rounded and healthy humanity. There is also a pathological end to the homosexuality spectrum. It consists in the fear, the terror, the scorn of, aversion to, and cutting off from intimate and bonded affection of the woman in the case of male homosexuals, and the man in the case of female homosexuals. This is the twist. Its roots, as we have seen, are traceable to traumatic events in the life of the foetus or infant.

But while we speak of this as a twist or deviation of the line of loving trust, it needs to be pointed out that many men and women have undergone a *total* blocking off of bodily loving. The homosexual person is at least capable of loving one half of the human race. There are many in authority, making pronouncements about human life and the nature of loving, who have never been able to accept a world of real people with real bodies and real relationships. They live shut away in their minds, outside their bodies, unaware of the sensations and feelings that provide the basis for the 'one-flesh' mystery. They may marry, have intercourse without tenderness, and become parents who cannot hug or be hugged by their children. They are people who were driven by the primitive traumas to split off the mind from the crushed and tortured body. They jettisoned their bodies in the womb or at birth as part of the evil world of mother, flesh, guts, genitals, women and embodied men. They have taken refuge in an ivory tower of mental and spiritual superiority. In New Testament times they were called gnostics. Their secret scorn of the bodily intimacies of all human relationships, whether with men or women, is an even deeper and more drastic injury to the line of love and trust than the homosexual's. The links in the latter from self to body are still intact.

There are, then, two false ways of counsel which the pastoral counsellor needs to avoid. One is, like that of the homophile clubs, to come out and become monosexual, the other that of those church-men, who speak from the aridities of their schizoid fear of all the bodily life of persons, to avoid bodily loving. The latter forget Christ's constant affirmation of the goodness of appropriate touch-ing and tender loving holding. Church people can do the devil's work of destroying, not sins, but men and women, when condemn-ing what they do not understand.

So pastoral counselling has an important part to play in helping clients to accept homosexual tenderness as a great gift of God. It is a rich part of each person's humanity. Healthy development in a man involves the integration of feminity – qualities more typically shown by women – and homosexuality will also involve working at the resistances to trusting and being close to the opposite sex, so as to make eventual tender commitment possible, to women as well as men in the case of a male homosexual, to men as well as to women in the case of a female homosexual.

To stress the problem of homosexuality, as I do here, might appear to make it into *the* problem, as indeed it is for many in the Church today. But that is to forget that it is only one of many problems which are part and parcel of our being hurt and human beings. Counsellors and clients, Christians and those who profess no belief, homosexuals and heterosexuals, can all learn from a remark of Freud's: 'In matters of sexuality at present we are all, every one of us, hypocrites, whether we be ill or well.'

CHAPTER 11

Infatuation and the Divine

Clouds of Glory at the Dawn of Being

The exalted, unitive joys of life in the womb break out in adult life in many ways.

When, for instance, a man is infatuated with a woman, he feels, as he gazes on and touches his new-found source of untold joy and ecstasy, that he is in direct contact with the immortal 'god' Eros. By means of his own projection on to her of the blessed feminine archetypes, he feels himself to be in direct contact with the very sources of beauty and eternal love. And no doubt in one sense he is. The assurances of immortality, eternity, omnipotence etc. with which he *is* in direct contact through his perfect lady, are real enough to destroy whatever else in the world of time and history and domesticity he ever promised to be faithful to and to protect with his life. He feels that he has here found 'life', infinitely attractive and seductive. Previous ethical commitments have relatively little hold on him. 'God' is inseparable from these amazing, transporting delights. His whole body is tingling with the truth of it. The recklessness of total abandonment seems justified. She is the pearl of great price for which, surely, the wise man of the Gospel parable will sell all. The wife and children he leaves behind seem no more than a mess of pottage, readily to be bartered for so immortal a prize.

God, the Father of Christ, enters through the Son into time and history. Christ upheld the honest domesticity this man is now despising. Duration of commitment and covenant are central to Christian spirituality. So the question is raised, what is this intoxicating quality of life with the infinitely exciting woman he now worships? 'I thee worship', in the Christian marriage service had always sounded rather extravagant or a bit blasphemous. But now 'worship' is the only word to match the feeling. Man is made for the worship of 'God' and why should not a woman be the vehicle of that worship? The Hindus and the Greeks, the Egyptians and the pagans have as many female deities as male. The question arises for the natural man, 'why should not this woman be liberated to be "God" for me, to command my total loyalty?'

I look back on the men who have shared this shattering experience with me while still in the midst of it. They have come because its enthralment has not totally taken over. Some vestige of the old sense of direction remained, some realization of the loss of face in society should it be known, and of pain to the existing family when it is 'acted out'. It is a tug-of-war between *immediacy* (in the Kierkegaardian sense) of feeling totally dependent on the love object outside himself, without whom a bottomless pit of despair yawns beneath him, and *reflection* in which he is able to step back from this totally regressed, actually primitive 'Child' self, to gain some hold with his 'Adult' self on the commitments he has acquired during a lifetime.

Here I have chosen to speak of this infatuation as it strikes married men, the fascinating 'god' being a 'goddess'. But, of course, it hits married women, either through some other breathtaking man, or a matchless woman. When a lesbian attachment breaks a marriage the same bemused adoration takes priority over the dull tie. Male homosexual partnerships are also made and broken at the command of this imperious passion.

As counsellors we must be able to feel the immense force and absolute certainty that this eruption via projection brings to the individual, of being with, and in the enjoyment of, the immortal 'gods' men have worshipped from time immemorial. To fail in this is to fail in empathy, the *sine qua non* of helpful contact with anyone. The captivated man or woman must feel that we can understand his enthusiasm for this wonderful sense of liberation and exaltation. Good in itself, it is a 'good' long imprisoned in his inner Garden of Eden, now somehow escaped through the garden gate. If, when it came upon us, we were able to recognize its sources in an authentic, actual past, recoverable in its true context, both personal, before birth and after, and archetypal, via our genetic inheritance, we could enjoy it without harm. It was a common experience among the contemplative nuns whom St Theresa of Ávila counselled. They were exalted to the seventh heaven by its recovery. The well-instructed among them focused it upon God the Father, or God the Son, at times upon the Blessed Virgin. St Theresa's level-headed advice was to enjoy it while it lasted, but to attach no particular importance to it. Above all, this did not indicate some special favour of God to some specially devout nun. The last thing to do was to extrapolate any kind of theology out of it. It was just one of those things, those happy things that we enjoy while they last, but we must on no account hang on to or desire deliberately to regain. Correctly put in its context (the sensations and the emotions of primal relationships) the whole can be enjoyed with praise and thankfulness, with no attempt to transform it from what it rightly is (a brief excursion on one of the trailing clouds of glory that accompanied the dawn of being) into a goal to be striven for and attained again and again in life. It is no doubt part of that great gift to our humanity of the cosmic Christ by whom the worlds and our humanity were made. But our redemption is in God's search for us, his call and his election. Our salvation is not in our search for exalted experiences. God reigns by Jesus Christ and his Cross. He did not seek to retain the exaltation of the Mount of Transfiguration. He set his face steadfastly away from there to go to Jerusalem. We court disaster if we do otherwise. The disaster is in the delusion. The overpowering illusion is in its seeming total rightness.

The Ethical Issues

The counsellor cannot be ethically indifferent in this matter. It is of sufficiently common occurrence for it to be necessary that he should understand what he makes of it. I remember that in the early days of the Balint groups for general practitioners, this precise problem came up. The puzzled doctor brought to the group the case of a married patient of his who had fallen in love with an attractive married neighbour and was well into an affair. What should he advise her to do? Soon the GPs were at one another's throats – in the moderate way the English have – one maintaining that she should get back to her husband and stop messing about, another asking what she was waiting for. If they were both in love the obvious thing was to get on with it. It's love that matters, hang the consequences. The first came back at the second in indignant protest at such 'permissiveness'.

Counsellors do not have the confidence of many GPs in prescribing this or that behaviour like a bottle of medicine, or conduct like a dose of salts. But in subtler ways, counsellors cannot avoid making value-judgements, which is a way of taking sides. We do that best by being not just fair to, but in a subjective way enthusiastic about, the side we quietly hope the other will not take. Objectivity is in the person of Christ and the word of God. Idolatry is still idolatry. To swear life faithfulness to 'Neighbour Number One' and then to disappoint her because her presence hinders our proliferating passion is a mark of infirmity, not of strength and godliness. The spirit of the age approves, but that never has been a guide to the wise, and of counsellors some wisdom is expected.

At least we do well to know our way about this problem, but not so as to take the client's decision for him or her. We might aspire to be a capable guide. The journey is dangerous and difficult either way. The counsellor needs to be an expert in the critique of existing ways. Never is this such that he tries to impose his will upon the other. The main purpose is to be able to recognize where the other is, in the complex roles that join the internal world with the external world.

If the Bible, especially the Christocentric anthropology of the New Testament, is right about man, then the way must be based on the guidelines of scripture. The Christian counsellor needs continually to be mindful of these guidelines. Most human crises and conflicts are, in one way or another, related to these.

Of course, the obviously bad, the corrupt, socially impossible vices are the same for both Christian and non-Christian. The roads to these have common warning signs so long as civilization lasts. The first chapter of Paul's letter to the Romans is a harrowing picture of the perversion that follows when the ways to godliness and god-centredness are despised.

For although they knew God they did not honour him as God or give thanks to him, but they became futile in their thinking and their senseless minds were darkened. Claiming to be wise, they became fools and exchanged the glory of the immortal God for images resembling mortal man, or birds or animals or reptiles.

> Therefore God gave them up in the lusts of their hearts to impurity, to the dishonouring of their bodies among themselves, because they exchanged the truth about God for a lie and worshipped and served the creature rather than the Creator (Rom. 1:21-5 R.S.V.).

Paul makes it clear that the proper context for the understanding of the deep mysteries of human personality and of divine purpose is the loving fellowship of those who have been drawn into the Body of Christ:

> That their hearts may be encouraged as they are knit together in love, to have all the riches of assured understanding and the knowledge of God's mystery, of Christ, in whom are hid all the treasures of wisdom and knowledge. . . . As therefore you received Christ Jesus the Lord, so live in him, rooted and built up in him and established in the faith, just as you were taught, abounding in thanksgiving. See to it that no one makes a prey of you by philosophy and empty deceit, according to human tradition, according to the elemental spirits of the universe, and not according to Christ. For in him the whole fullness of the deity dwells bodily, and you have come to fullness of life in him. (Col. 2:2–3, 6–10 R.S.V.).

The Invasion of the Divine

Yet there are times when the sudden heat of a devouring passion in the form of a bolt-from-the-blue infatuation, calling a person to throw up all and follow 'the star', comes as a welcome shaking of sadly inadequate foundations. Some people's lives have had their foundations laid in the rubbish dump of cultural left-overs and the family throw-outs for several generations. They have never penetrated down to the solid ground even of their own perceptions of reality or to genuine feelings of their own about life.

There are those whose only concern is that this man or woman get back into line. He or she must cool off this unaccustomed ardour, must recognize that the mediocrity into which marital life settles down in middle-class society is the most that can be expected of it. Romance is for romantic novels or the television. It is to be indulged in only vicariously, in fantasies of identification with the hero and the heroine. Then go to bed with your wife or husband, and imagine both of you as other than you are.

A counsellor, especially if he or she is to be relied upon to take a safe, churchy line, has, in the view of such people, only one task: to prick the bubble and deflate this balloon. If, by tomorrow, this hot passion of a heart-sick lover can become, by skilled counselling, as cold as if it had never been, so much the better. If he returns to the safe, tepid waters of a dull, domestic co-existence, the counsellor will have done a good job. I have often been very aware of these expectations surrounding me.

But then some awkward texts come to mind, inviting you to consider this case in their strangely blinding light. There are the words of the Son of man in the Revelation to St John. They come from the radiant figure 'from [whose] mouth issued a sharp two-edged sword, and his face was like the sun shining in full strength' (Rev. 1:16 R.S.V.). They are the words to the Church in Laodicea:

> The words of the Amen, the faithful and true witness, the beginning of God's creation. 'I know your works : you are neither cold nor hot. Would that you were cold or hot! So, because you are lukewarm, and neither cold nor hot, I will spew you out of my mouth. For you say, I am rich, I have prospered, and I need nothing; not knowing that you are wretched, pitiable, poor, blind, and naked. Therefore I counsel you to buy from me gold refined by fire. (Rev. 3:14–18 R.S.V.)

The lukewarmness of the Laodiceans, which nauseates God, is a basic ingredient of that denial of passion which leads to a pseudo-servility in which those who are embedded in it feel smug and self-satisfied. Something with the violence of passion has to come along to shake them out of this blindness. With the scales removed they can have eyes to see that, under God, the destiny of man is an election to an unending glory, an expanding lover-beloved relationship. The pressuring culture of which he is a compliant part is not greater, or more long lasting than he is. He will outlive it. But he must begin, now, to live outside it, or the new road to life is never begun.

Suppose I am in the presence of a man who is still in a fiery furnace, burnt up with longing for his lady-love. This is a 'divine' invasion. Let us not quarrel here about the difference between the theological and the popular use of 'divine' as an adjective. A certain

kind of morality strives to dub this whole excursion into passion as
'godlessness'. Our text indicates a greater godlessness in a contented
self-cosseting mentality, moulded by mediocrity. The counsellor's
task is to perceive the moment or fragment of truth in this grand
illusion. Its value is not in pursuing it for itself. That would be
further delusion. Its value is in its ability to broaden and deepen
greatly the experiential dimensions of a personality. It is in its
power to break up monotony and arouse expectations of something
better, something more alive, joyful, vivacious, exciting and glorious, that we come to value it in the divine economy.

Anything that can begin the process of disrupting a deadly drift
through life, plodding and snoozing, complying and preening oneself
by turns, is a potential Godsend. One of the cardinal principles of
Christian pastoral counselling is that 'everything is usable'. With
the gold of Christ's fiery trial brought alongside him, our infatuated
man may begin to purchase, from the shared experience, that 'gold
refined by fire' which the two-edged sword-tongued Son of man
counsels here. It is our task to make clear that this transformation
is possible, and how it is possible.

This person has never before noticed the glory of God in his
handiwork, the glory of a man made in his image, or of a woman
bearing a reflection of his radiance. God is not directly present in
his handiwork. If our closed-in lives are broken up to see, not only
the wonder of the infinitely attractive other person, but also the
even greater compelling authority of the ethical to restrain our
chasing after it, we enter a whole new world; but God is still not
directly present to us. No one uses irony to better effect than Søren
Kierkegaard to shock us into recognizing the contrast between our
clipped wings, the flightless, pedestrian existence with which we are
pressured to be contented, and the 'hope of our calling' to glory by
Christ Jesus.

Is not God so unnoticeable, so secretly present in his works, that
a man might very well live his entire life, be married, become
known and respected as citizen, father and captain of the hunt,
without ever having discovered God in his works, and without
ever having received any impression of the infinitude of the ethical. . . . He would never do anything first, and he would never
have any opinion which he did not first know that others had.
. . . He would perhaps also see God in nature when in company

with others who saw God; he would be a pleasant society man – and yet he would have been deceived by the direct nature of his relationship to the truth, to the ethical, and to God. . . If one were to delineate such a man experimentally, he would be a satire upon the human. It is really the God-relationship that makes a man a man, and yet he would be lacking this. . . At the end of his life, one would have to say that one thing had escaped him; his consciousness had taken no note of God. If God could have permitted a direct relationship, he would doubtless have taken notice. If God, for example, had taken on the figure of a very rare and tremendously large green bird with a red beak, sitting on a tree on the mound, and perhaps even whistling in an unheard of manner – then the society man would have been able to get his eyes open, and for the first time in his life would be first.[1]

Kierkegaard's portrayal of this man without inwardness, is of one who is no more than a lifeless reflection of other people's patterns and opinions. 'Man', as Pascal wrote, 'is born an original and dies a copy.'[2] He is in 'direct contact' of a sort, but only with travestied and devalued versions of what God is in his relation to man. Now, in this unruly falling-in-love, he has had an overwhelming experience that has lifted him out of the rut. Within himself he is at least sure of something, by the self-evident truth of his own strong, and for the first time indisputable, subjective feelings. He is taken over by them, lifted by the scruff of the neck, one might say, out of himself, and out of the social matrix to which he had looked slavishly for esteem in return for compliance. This is too precious a moment not to be seized upon in the service of a truth greater than itself.

So the first obstacle to be overcome in counselling is likely to be that of the 'transference' expectation. Our man will expect to hear from the counsellor the voice of the 'Parent', condemning, deprecating, warning, with nothing good to say about the whole episode. His defences will be up to defend it. Before he has wakened up to the fact that we are speaking in an Adult way to his Adult, he is likely to mistake our positive evaluation of his experience, and the lack of a note of condemnation in our voice, as our siding with the Child in its enthusiasm for this discovery of unimagined glory. He may take it that we approve heartily of his relationship with this

---

[1] S. Kierkegaard, Works, reference untraced.
[2] B. Pascal. *Pensées*, J. M. Dent and Sons, 1973.

'direct' representative of immortal Love itself. But our empathy with the Child's breakthrough into archetypal joys is not the same as a compliant sympathy such as would totally share his exaltation and support the resolution to carry it through. Somehow, we must communicate that difference. Eventually, if a sound Adult-to-Adult relationship can be made, the work will have some .eal chance of success. We are able then to appeal from Philip 'drunk' to Philip 'sober', without going by way of Philip 'bad'.

In the passage quoted, Kierkegaard hints that never having emerged from the ethical constraints of parental influence, this citizen and father had not only never discovered the glory of God in His handiwork, he had, by the same token, passed through life 'without ever having received any impression of the infinitude of the ethical'. He has now broken out of the social shell or cultural cocoon. He is snatched up into an all-engrossing passion that stretches him into dimensions of being and commitment that threaten all the conventional ethics of his quite correct upbringing. 'Therefore shall a man leave his father and mother and cleave to his wife' (Matt. 19:5). His old marriage had been such a family affair, with the parents on both sides so pleased to see them safely wed. All that talk about 'leaving and cleaving' seemed over-dramatic at the time, and just not applicable. But now he feels, in the deepest fibre of his nature, aglow with the kind of adoration and longing that for the first time makes sense of the drama of leaving and cleaving. He passionately desires to leave his wife, and to cleave – elsewhere.

He has not explored this road far as 'a Christian' before he collides with the Word of Christ about adultery, even to the extent of looking 'on a woman to lust after her' (Matt. 5:28 A.V.). For the first time in his life, whichever way he ultimately decides to go, he has 'received an impression of the infinitude of the ethical'.

The counsellor may meet the woman in question or see her photograph. She usually has youth on her side. She still enjoys all that age has still to take away from her in looks. Beyond that, the cooler eye of the observer often senses that the beauty the love-sick man worships is in his own eye as the beholder. Most of what delights him as he looks at her is derived from his own inner endowment, projected upon her. His own blessed and wholly adorable primal or archetypal image of the ideal feminine figure has, by some quirk of fortune or fate, fastened upon her. He thinks, indeed he is totally convinced that it all belongs to her, and that to lose her is to lose all. In fact, he could withdraw these projections without loss to himself. He would only be taking back his own. But to convince a man or a woman of that fact is never easy. Indeed, to make the attempt directly is to forget all that one has learnt in personal experience about the force and finality of projection, particularly when support from ordinary sources has been withdrawn from the ego. Self-criticism weakens, defensiveness begins.

If, at times, projection seems to account for most of the fixation, at others one is aghast at the genuine contrast between a wife who has become sharp, bitter and shrewish, and a lovely woman who genuinely loves this married man, who flowers in her presence. Aghast, because the pastoral counsellor has no authority to dispense with the word of Christ who, in the final judgement, has the last word. Christ's sovereign and final word is in the forgiveness of sins, but there is a fearful responsibility in becoming an accessory to making a decision to sin. Though in this chapter I have been principally concerned with projection and fixation, there is another set of tight corners, where reality factors in the marriage make their own contribution.

CHAPTER 12

Attending to Ourselves

St Paul, writing to Timothy about how to manage himself in a leadership role unusual for so young a man, presses all kinds of advice on him. When he summarizes his instruction there are two strands to it 'Attend to yourself' or 'Take heed to yourself' and 'Attend, or take heed to the teaching.'

'Tight corners' or 'critical incidents' will continue to beset us for as long as we continue in any kind of helping relationship. The probability is that, just as we needed more help than we could give during our apprenticeship, we shall need to accept the same imbalance again in our retirement and ageing. Between the two dependencies there can be a long period of generativity when we are able to receive and to give generously. There are less 'critical incidents' that take us by surprise, and we have evidently gained some skill in negotiating 'tight corners'. After the struggles to reach this plateau we feel entitled to relax and 'eat the fruits of our labours'. On the way up we had to attend to our teachers and to the state of play in the game in which we determined to succeed. Now let others attend to us.

This is a constant temptation for professional helpers, 'I've come up the hard way. Now attend to me. Let me teach you how.' Implicitly this means, 'Meet my needs for recognition. Meet my need to be a teacher whose pupils get on, a helper whose clients do well.'

The helper is helping himself to the relationship. It must now minister to *his or her* needs. The counsellee, falling into the collusive trap, thrusts aside the agenda with which he or she came to you, namely the hope of meeting someone to attend to *his or her* own needs, and begins, anxiously to attend to yours. If you are anxious about 'failing', this will come over as an expectation, even an insistence, that your 'treatment' be successful. You both define success in terms of a reduction in the number and severity of symptoms, so the client is tempted to conceal half his or her trouble so as not to increase yours.

'Not disappointing parents or teachers' has been, and will no doubt remain a motive for working hard and doing well in education. The needs of the teacher and pupil for 'success' are sufficiently congruent. But this will not do in a profession so beset by intrinsic and necessary paradoxes as counselling.

The teaching which is the basis of our practice asks for much the same commitment whether we derive it from R. R. Carkhuff's classical studies pinpointing the primary need to attend to the counsellee, with empathy, respect, genuineness, concreteness, confrontation and immediacy, or from the dynamics of Christian discipleship, and the embodying in ourselves of Christ's total, costly attentiveness to others in their abysmal needs. The helper must first have his or her own needs met elsewhere. Otherwise he or she will not be free enough from unacknowledged needs within and will, in a clandestine way, be seeking to have them met by the client.

The right proportions must be observed or there is darkness where light was sought. It is all too easy for our blindness, as helpers who have failed to attend to ourselves, to lead our clients into a similar blindness, so that they too, do not attend to themselves either, but to meeting our unacknowledged needs. It is a typical collusion, such as society loves to look down on with amusement, for we all do it, most of all those who would be teachers. 'The sins of teachers are the teachers of sins'.

Attend to yourself. But 'Who is myself?' is a question that battles with 'Who is my neighbour?' for priority and penetrating difficulty. Attend to which voices, the Parent voices, the Child voices, or the Adult voice that attends to self and neighbour in some proportion approximating to justice? But what is justice, in a world where there is so much injustice still in the pipeline, the umbilical or parental pipeline, still feeding the injustice and distress of decades ago into the personality struggles of adults, messing up their best efforts? *Distributive* justice, fair shares for all, is not enough. *Retributive* justice tends to punish those to whom, all things considered, *restitutive* justice should first have given a long run of 'luck' or a renewal in a loving relationship that would have cost someone all they had to give.

Counsellors are not in the business of mere distributive justice, much less of retributive justice. Theirs is a vocation to *restitutive* justice. So we are invited to help carry heavy burdens that we have not laid on our clients. If we suffer under a corner of the weight that crushes our clients, we are part of a restitutive justice that is at work in the world.

At first this can collude with the fantasy with which we may well have rewarded ourselves during a tough period in the womb, that we were doing something significant by our care of mother, to mitigate the sorrows of her in whom we were coming to life. But that care of the mother by the foetus in the womb, the foetal-therapist syndrome, is to silence one's own needs, while attending to her distress, in order to lessen the pain for oneself of having to be invaded by hers. There is a very powerful scripted message imprinted here, against first obeying the injunction 'Attend to yourself'. We have to make everybody else happy first. So we collect the pay-off of our self-imposed martyrdom and pat ourselves on the back that the virtuous motto 'Others first' has been observed. The snag is, we import this radical injustice into our counselling. We seem to be saying to the client, 'See how assiduously I am attending to you' and maybe we are. But as part of what kind of a dynamic input-output chart? That is crucial. Are we attending in order to be attended to by a grateful client? Or is this attending the outflow and expression of the satisfactoriness of the ways in which we have been accepted and sustained by the freely given attention of others? The former perpetuates a subtle kind of injustice. The latter establishes a new kind of justice because our client, attended to out of our freedom and sufficiency, is free to do what he or she likes with the offer. The double bind of collusive relationships is abolished.

So my attending to myself in this vocation, means attending to the sources of my ability to be consistently part of a group able to offer relationships in which restitutive and reparative justice can be experienced by those who have lacked them. On behalf of a creation that has miscarried and on behalf of a society and families that have passed on and perpetuated injustice to this hurt person, I am there to apologize. I invite their forgiveness by hearing the anger of their protest against injustices without reproach. The message of my being there is the one God gave so powerfully to the Lady Julian of Norwich, 'I saw no blame'.

If the Cross of Christ says anything to the afflicted, who suffered first, and fatally for their trust, in the first trimester of life in the womb, about the forgiveness of their sins it is that *he is God, begging their forgiveness* for the hurts caused by the sins of the fathers, funnelled into them by the distress of the mothers. This theme, of Christ as the innocent, just man, as the Lamb taken from the flock to have the sins of others laid on his head, sharing the lot of all the innocent afflicted, this is the deepest and earliest level of meaning in the suffering of the Son of God.

This metaphor creates a new world of relationships. What we suffered early so disrupted all the meaningful relationships upon which meaning itself depended, as to render life hereafter meaningless and not worth the living. It can be repaired only by the suffering's happening again, in full recall of its pain, but within a shared relationship which is determined not to be disrupted. The suffering is the same, and more may follow, but the meaning of it, how it is perceived, is transformed by the new metaphor: 'He is with me; they are with me; I am not alone.' So much of the horror of primal affliction lies in the solitariness of the suffering. With someone else there, in whose face I can see every familiar agony of my own soul, the intensity and bearableness of the suffering are quite changed.

Index of Names

Index of Subjects

abortion, 41; attempted, 30, 38, 40, 41, 42, 90
abyss, 51, 76, 173
acceptance, 24, 35, 64, 80, 121, 123, 142, 147; unwise, 79; lost, 104, 116
acting-out, 132, 163; inhibited, 133
action, 64, 92
adolescence, 8, 11, 24, 54, 82, 87, 125, 140, 152
adult state, 10–11, 24, 57
adultery, 142, 170
affliction, 14, 15, 16, 17, 21, 27–31, 44, 46, 47, 49, 51, 52, 54, 130, 134, 137, 148, 175
agony, 67, 95
agoraphobia, 88, 127
allergy, 32, 34
anger (see rage), 15, 23, 33, 80, 96, 98–109, 116, 133, 142, 143, 174; hidden, 103, 105; justifiable, 129
anguish, 13, 27, 30, '32, 42, 52, 68, 79, 101
anorexia nervosa, 151, 152
anxiety, 55, 103, 121; of commitment, 55; of separation, 19, 51, 102; symptoms of, 112; existential, 122; intra-uterine, 16, 21; professional, 73
archetypes, 8, 162f, 170
asphyxia (see suffocation), 18, 51
assimiliation, 28, 120, 145

association, 35, 74
assumptions, 40, 49, 79, 87
attention, 9, 25, 30, 73, 79, 95, 132, 173
authenticity, 84, 87–97
authority, authorities 49, 61, 62, 89, 90, 91, 114, 125, 146, 168
awareness, 46, 63, 65, 73, 97, 103, 138, 145

badness, 32, 33, 51, 52, 88, 145, 155
befriending, 115, 143
behaviourism, 85, 116
being itself, 63; ground of, 46, 63
betrayal, 80, 150
bioenergetic therapy, 7, 10
biofeedback, 35, 36
birth, 8, 13, 55, 94, 128, 141, 147
birth trauma, 2, 3, 4, 17–20, 24, 30, 51, 66, 101, 138, 154; and depression, 44, 45
bitterness, 129, 130, 131, 133, 134
blackness, invasive, 17, 31, 32, 51, 131
blame, 52, 88, 133, 135; no, 77, 81, 90, 136, 175
blastocystic phase, 15, 23, 29, 63; bliss, 40, 65; blessedness, 63, 65, 66
blood, 5, 36, 45